# A Charles Williams Reader

*Descent into Hell,*
*Many Dimensions*
*&*
*War in Heaven*

WILLIAM B. EERDMANS PUBLISHING COMPANY
GRAND RAPIDS, MICHIGAN / CAMBRIDGE, U.K.

*Descent into Hell*
© 1937 Charles Williams
© 1949 Pelligrini & Cudahy

*Many Dimensions*
© 1931 Charles Williams
© 1949 Pellegrini & Cudahy

*War in Heaven*
© 1930 Charles Williams
© 1949 Pellegrini & Cudahy

This edition published in 2000 by
Wm. B. Eerdmans Publishing Co.
255 Jefferson Ave. S.E., Grand Rapids, Michigan 49503 /
P.O. Box 163, Cambridge CB3 9PU U.K.

Printed in the United States of America

04 03 02 01 00    5 4 3 2 1

ISBN 0-8028-3906-1 (cloth : alk. paper)

www.eerdmans.com

# DESCENT INTO HELL

# DESCENT INTO HELL

by

CHARLES WILLIAMS

WILLIAM B. EERDMANS PUBLISHING COMPANY
GRAND RAPIDS, MICHIGAN

PHOTOLITHOPRINTED BY EERDMANS PRINTING COMPANY
GRAND RAPIDS, MICHIGAN, UNITED STATES OF AMERICA

# CONTENTS

*Chapter One*

# THE MAGUS ZOROASTER

"It undoubtedly needs", Peter Stanhope said, "a final pulling together, but there's hardly time for that before July, and if you're willing to take it as it is, why——" He made a gesture of presentation and dropped his eyes, thus missing the hasty reciprocal gesture of gratitude with which Mrs. Parry immediately replied on behalf of the dramatic culture of Battle Hill. Behind and beyond her the culture, some thirty faces, unessentially exhibited to each other by the May sunlight, settled to attention—naturally, efficiently, critically, solemnly, reverently. The grounds of the Manor House expanded beyond them; the universal sky sustained the whole. Peter Stanhope began to read his play.

Battle Hill was one of the new estates which had been laid out after the war. It lay about thirty miles north of London and took its title from the more ancient name of the broad rise of ground which it covered. It had a quiet ostentation of comfort and culture. The poor, who had created it, had been as far as possible excluded, nor (except as hired servants) were they permitted to experience the bitterness of others' stairs. The civil wars which existed there, however bitter, were conducted with all bourgeois propriety. Politics, religion, art, science, grouped themselves, and courteously competed for numbers and reputation. This summer, however, had seen a spectacular triumph of drama, for it had become known that Peter Stanhope had consented to allow the restless talent of the Hill to produce his latest play.

He was undoubtedly the most famous inhabitant. He was a cadet of that family which had owned the Manor House, and he had bought it back from more recent occupiers, and himself settled in it before the war. He had been able to do this because he was something more than a cadet of good family, being also a poet in the direct English line, and so much after the style of his greatest predecessor that he made money out of poetry. His name was admired by his contemporaries and respected by the young. He had even imposed modern plays in verse on the London theatre, and two of them tragedies at that, with a farce or two, and histories for variation and pleasure. He was the kind of figure who might be more profitable to his neighbourhood dead than alive; dead, he would have given it a shrine; alive, he deprecated worshippers. The young men at the estate office made a refined publicity out of his privacy; the name of Peter Stanhope would be whispered without comment. He endured the growing invasion with a great deal of good humour, and was content to see the hill of his birth become a suburb of the City, as in another sense it would always be. There was, in that latest poetry, no contention between the presences of life and of death; so little indeed that there had been a contention in the *Sunday Times* whether Stanhope were a pessimist or an optimist. He himself said, in reply to an interviewer's question, that he was an optimist and hated it.

Stanhope, though the most glorious, was not the only notorious figure of the Hill. There was Mr. Lawrence Wentworth, who was the most distinguished living authority on military history (perhaps excepting Mr. Aston Moffatt). Mr. Wentworth was not in the garden on that afternoon. Mrs. Catherine Parry was; it was she who would produce the play, as in many places and at many times she had produced others. She sat near Stanhope now, almost as tall as he, and with more active though not brighter eyes. They were part of that presence which was so necessary to her profession. Capacity which, in her nature, had reached the extreme of active life, seemed in him to have entered the contemplative, so much had his art become a thing of his soul. Where, in their own separate private affairs, he interfered so little as almost to seem inefficient, she was so efficient as almost to seem interfering.

In the curve of women and men beyond her, other figures, less generally famous, sat or lay as the depth of their chairs induced them. There were rising young men, and a few risen and retired old. There were ambitious young women and sullen young women and loquacious young women. They were all attentive, though, as a whole, a little disappointed. They had understood that Mr. Stanhope had been writing a comedy, and had hoped for a modern comedy. When he had been approached, however, he had been easy but firm. He had been playing with a pastoral; if they would like a pastoral, it was very much at their service. Hopes and hints of modern comedies were unrealized: it was the pastoral or nothing. They had to be content. He consented to read it to them; he would not do more. He declined to make suggestions for the cast; he declined to produce. He would like, for his own enjoyment, to come to some of the rehearsals, but he made it clear that he had otherwise no wish to interfere. Nothing—given the necessity of a pastoral—could be better; the production would have all the advantage of his delayed death without losing any advantage of his prolonged life. As this became clear, the company grew reconciled. They gazed and listened, while from the long lean figure, outstretched in its deck-chair, there issued the complex intonation of great verse. Never negligible, Stanhope was often neglected; he was everyone's second thought, but no one's first. The convenience of all had determined this afternoon that he should be the first, and his neat mass of grey hair, his vivid glance, that rose sometimes from the manuscript, and floated down the rows, and sank again, his occasional friendly gesture that seemed about to deprecate, but always stopped short, received the concentration of his visitors, and of Mrs. Parry, the chief of his visitors.

It became clear to Mrs. Parry, as the afternoon and the voice went on, that the poet had been quite right when he had said that the play needed pulling together. "It's all higgledy-piggledy," she said to herself, using a word which a friend had once applied to a production of the *Tempest*, and in fact to the *Tempest* itself. Mrs. Parry thought that this pastoral was, in some ways, rather like the *Tempest*. Mr. Stanhope, of course, was not as good as Shakespeare, because Shakespeare was the greatest English poet, so that Stanhope wasn't. But there was a something. To begin with, it had no title beyond *A Pastoral*. That was unsatisfactory. Then the plot was incredibly loose. It was of no particular time and no particular place, and to any cultured listener it seemed to have little bits of everything and everybody put in at odd moments. The verse was undoubtedly Stanhope's own, of his latest, most heightened, and most epigrammatic style, but now and then all kinds of reminiscences moved in it. Once, during the second act, the word *pastiche* floated through Mrs. Parry's mind, but went away again on her questioning whether a *pastiche* would be worth the trouble of production. There was a Grand Duke in it, who had a beautiful daughter, and this daughter either escaped from the palace or was abducted —anyhow, she came into the power of a number of brigands; and then there was a woodcutter's son who frequently burned leaves, and he and the princess fell in love, and there were two farmers who were at odds, and the Grand Duke turned up in disguise, first in a village and then in the forest, through which also wandered an escaped bear, who spoke the most complex verse of all, excepting the Chorus. The Chorus had no kind of other name; at first Mrs. Parry thought they might be villagers, then, since they were generally present in the forest, she thought they might be trees, or perhaps (with a vague reminiscence of *Comus*) spirits. Stanhope had not been very helpful; he had alluded to them as an experiment. By the end of the reading, it was clear to Mrs. Parry that it was very necessary to decide what exactly this Chorus was to be.

She had discouraged discussion of the play during the intervals between the four acts, and as soon as it was over tea was served. If, however, the poet hoped to get away from discussion by means of tea he was mistaken. There was a little hesitation over the correct word; fantastic was dangerous, and poetic both unpopular and supererogatory, though both served for variations on idyllic, which was Mrs. Parry's choice and won by lengths. As she took her second cup of tea, however, she began to close. She said: "Yes, idyllic, Mr. Stanhope, and so significant!"

"It's very good of you," Stanhope murmured. "But you see I was right about revision—the plot must seem very loose."

Mrs. Parry waved the plot up into benevolence. "But there are a few points," she went on. "The Chorus now. I don't think I follow the Chorus."

"The Chorus *could* be omitted," Stanhope said. "It's not absolutely necessary to a presentation."

Before Mrs. Parry could answer, a young woman named Adela Hunt, sitting close by, leant forward. She was the leader of the younger artistic party, who were not altogether happy about Mrs. Parry. Adela had some thoughts of taking up production herself as her life-work, and it would have been a great advantage to have started straight away with Peter Stanhope. But her following was not yet strong enough to deal with Mrs. Parry's reputation. She was determined, however, if possible, to achieve a kind of collaboration by means of correction. "O, we oughtn't to omit anything, ought we?" she protested. "A work of art can't spare anything that's a part of it."

"My dear," Mrs. Parry said, "you must consider your audience. What will the audience make of the Chorus?"

"It's for them to make what they can of it," Adela answered.

"We can only give them a symbol. Art's always symbolic, isn't it?"

Mrs. Parry pursed her lips. "I wouldn't say symbolic exactly," she said slowly. "It has a significance, of course, and you've got to convey that significance to the audience. We want to present it—to interpret."

As she paused, distracted by the presentation by the poet of two kinds of sandwiches, Adela broke in again.

"But, Mrs. Parry, how can one interpret a symbol? One can only *mass* it. It's all of a piece, and it's the total effect that creates the symbolical force."

"Significant, not symbolical," said Mrs. Parry firmly. "You mustn't play down to your audience, but you mustn't play away from them either. You must"—she gesticulated—"intertwine . . . harmonize. So you must make it easy for them to get into harmony. That's what's wrong with a deal of modern art; it refuses—it doesn't establish equilibrium with its audience or what not. In a pastoral play you must have equilibrium."

"But the equilibrium's in the *play*,"Adela urged again, "a balance of masses. Surely that's what drama is—a symbolical contrast of masses."

"Well," Mrs. Parry answered with infuriating tolerance, "I suppose you might call it that. But it's more effective to think of it as significant equilibrium—especially for a pastoral. However, don't let's be abstract. The question is, what's to be done about the Chorus? Had we better keep it in or leave it out? Which would you prefer, Mr. Stanhope?"

"I should prefer it in, if you ask me," Stanhope said politely. "But not to inconvenience the production."

"It seems to be in the forest so often," Mrs. Parry mused, dismissing cake. "There's the distant song in the first act, when the princess goes away from the palace, and the choric dialogue when. . . . It isn't Dryads, is it?"

A friend of Adela's, a massive and superb young man of

twenty-five, offered a remark. "Dryads would rather wreck the eighteenth century, wouldn't they?"

"Watteau," said a young lady near Adela. "You could have them period."

Mrs. Parry looked at her approvingly. "Exactly, my dear," she said. "A very charming fantasy it might be; we must take care it isn't precious—only period. But, Mr. Stanhope, you haven't told us—are they Dryads?"

"Actually," Stanhope answered, "as I told you, it's more an experiment than anything else. The main thing is—was— that they are non-human."

"Spirits?" said the Watteau young lady with a trill of pleasure.

"If you like," said Stanhope, "only not spiritual. Alive, but with a different life—even from the princess."

"Irony?" Adela exclaimed. "It's a kind of comment, isn't it, Mr. Stanhope, on futility? The forest and everything, and the princess and her lover—so transitory."

Stanhope shook his head. There was a story, invented by himself, that *The Times* had once sent a representative to ask for explanations about a new play, and that Stanhope, in his efforts to explain it, had found after four hours that he had only succeeded in reading it completely through aloud: "Which," he maintained, "*was* the only way of explaining it."

"No," he said now, "not irony. I think perhaps you'd better cut them out."

There was a moment's pause. "But we can't do that, Mr. Stanhope," said a voice; "they're important to the poetry, aren't they?" It was the voice of another young woman, sitting behind Adela. Her name was Pauline Anstruther, and, compared with Adela, she was generally silent. Now, after her quick question, she added hastily, "I mean—they come in when the princess and the wood-cutter come together, don't they?" Stanhope looked at her, and she felt as if his eyes had opened suddenly. He said, more slowly:

"In a way, but they needn't. We could just make it chance."

"I don't think that would be nearly as satisfactory," Mrs. Parry said. "I begin to see my way—the trees perhaps—leaves —to have the leaves of the wood all so helpful to the young people—so charming!"

"It's a terribly sweet idea," said the Watteau young lady. "And so true too!"

Pauline, who was sitting next her, said in an undertone: "True?"

"Don't you think so?" Watteau, whose actual name was Myrtle Fox, asked. "It's what I always feel—about trees and flowers and leaves and so on—they're so *friendly*. Perhaps you don't notice it so much; I'm rather mystic about nature. Like Wordsworth. I should love to spend *days* out with nothing but the trees and the leaves and the wind. Only somehow one never seems to have time. But I do believe they're all breathing in with us, and it's such a comfort—here, where there are so many trees. Of course, we've only to sink into ourselves to find peace—and trees and clouds and so on all help us. One never need be unhappy. Nature's so terribly good. Don't you think so, Mr. Stanhope?"

Stanhope was standing by, silent, while Mrs. Parry communed with her soul and with one or two of her neighbours on the possibilities of dressing the Chorus. He turned his head and answered, "That Nature is terribly good? Yes, Miss Fox. You do mean 'terribly'?"

"Why, certainly," Miss Fox said. "Terribly—dreadfully— very."

"Yes," Stanhope said again. "Very. Only—you must forgive me; it comes from doing so much writing, but when I say 'terribly' I think I mean 'full of terror'. A dreadful goodness."

"I don't see how goodness can be dreadful," Miss Fox said, with a shade of resentment in her voice. "If things are good they're not terrifying, are they?"

"It was you who said 'terribly'," Stanhope reminded her with a smile, "I only agreed."

"And if things are terrifying," Pauline put in, her eyes half-closed and her head turned away as if she asked a casual question rather of the world than of him, "can they be good?"

He looked down on her. "Yes, surely," he said, with more energy. "Are our tremors to measure the Omnipotence?"

"We'll have them in shades of green then," Mrs. Parry broke in, "light to dark, with rich gold sashes and embroidery running all over like twigs, and each one carrying a conventionalized bough—different lengths, I think. Dark gold stockings."

"To suggest the trunks?" asked Adela's friend, Hugh Prescott.

"Quite," Mrs. Parry said, and then hesitated. "I'm not sure—perhaps we'd better keep the leaf significances. When they're still—of course they could stand with their legs twined. . . ."

"What, with one another's?" Adela asked, in a conscious amazement.

"My dear child, don't be absurd," Mrs. Parry said. "Each pair of legs just crossed, so"—she interlaced her own.

"I could never stand still like that," Miss Fox said, with great conviction.

"You'd have your arms stretched out to people's shoulders on each side," Mrs. Parry said dubiously, "and a little gentle swaying wouldn't be inappropriate. But perhaps we'd better not risk it. Better have green stockings—we can manage some lovely groupings. Could we call them 'Chorus of Leaf-Spirits', Mr. Stanhope?"

"Sweet!" said Miss Fox. Adela, leaning back to Hugh Prescott, said in a very low voice, "I told you, Hugh, she'll ruin the whole thing. She's got no idea of mass. She ought to block it violently and leave it without a name. I wouldn't even have 'Chorus'. I hope he won't give way, but he's rather weak."

However, Stanhope was, in the politest language, declining to have anything of the sort. "Call it the Chorus," he said, "or if you like I'll try and find a name for the leader, and the rest can just dance and sing. But I'm afraid 'Leaf-Spirits' would be misleading."

"What about 'Chorus of Nature-Powers'?" asked Miss Fox, but Stanhope only said, smiling, "You will try and make the trees friendly," which no one quite understood, and shook his head again.

Prescott asked: "Incidentally, I suppose they will be women?"

Mrs. Parry had said, "O, of course, Mr. Prescott," before the question reached her brain. When it did, she added, "At least . . . I naturally took it for granted. . . . They are feminine, aren't they?"

Still hankering after mass, Adela said, "It sounds to me more like undifferentiated sex force," and ignored Hugh's murmur, "There isn't much fun in that."

"I don't know that they were meant to be either male or female," Stanhope said. "I told you they were more of an experiment in a different kind of existence. But whether men or women are most like that is another matter." He shed an apologetic smile on Mrs. Parry.

"If they're going to be leaves," Miss Fox asked, "couldn't they all *wear* huge green leaves, so that no one would know if they were wearing knee-breeches or skirts?"

There was a pause while everyone took this in, then Mrs. Parry said, very firmly, "I don't think that would answer," while Hugh Prescott said to Adela, "Chorus of Fig-leaves!"

"Why not follow the old pantomime or the present musical comedy," Stanhope asked, "and dress your feminine chorus in exquisite masculine costume? That's what Shakespeare did

with his heroines, as often as he could, and made a diagram of
something more sharp and wonderful than either. I don't
think you'll do better. Masculine voices—except boys—would
hardly do, nor feminine appearances."

Mrs. Parry sighed, and everyone contemplated the problem
again. Adela Hunt and Hugh Prescott discussed modernity
between themselves. Pauline, lying back, like Stanhope, in
her chair, was thinking of Stanhope's phrases, "a different
life", "a terrible good", and wondering if they were related,
if this Chorus over which they were spending so much trouble
were indeed an effort to shape in verse a good so alien as to be
terrifying. She had never considered good as a thing of terror,
and certainly she had not supposed a certain thing of terror
in her own secret life as any possible good. Nor now; yet there
had been an inhumanity in the great and moving lines of the
Chorus. She thought, with an anger generous in its origin but
proud and narrow in its conclusion, that not many of the
audience really cared for poetry or for Stanhope's poetry—
perhaps none but she. He was a great poet, one of a very
few, but what would he do if one evening he met himself
coming up the drive? *Doppelgänger*, the learned called it,
which was no comfort. Another poet had thought of it;
she had had to learn the lines at school, as an extra task
because of undone work:

> *The Magus Zoroaster, my dead child,*
> *Met his own image walking in the garden.*

She had never done the imposition, for she had had nightmares that night, after reading the lines, and had to go sick
for days. But she had always hated Shelley since for making it
so lovely, when it wasn't loveliness but black panic. Shelley
never seemed to suggest that the good might be terrible.
What would Peter Stanhope *do*? what could he? if he met
himself?

They were going: people were getting up and moving off. Everyone was being agreeably grateful to Stanhope for his lawn, his tea, and his poetry. In her fear of solitude she attached herself to Adela and Hugh and Myrtle Fox, who were all saying good-bye at once. As he shook hands he said casually: "You don't think they are?" and she did not immediately understand the reference to the measurement of Omnipotence by mortal tremors. Her mind was on Myrtle, who lived near her. She hated the pang of gratitude she felt, and hated it more because she despised Miss Fox. But at least she wouldn't be alone, and the thing she hated most only came, or had so far only come, when she was alone. She stuck close to Myrtle, listening to Adela as they went.

"Pure waste," Adela was saying. "Of course, Stanhope's dreadfully traditional"—how continually, Pauline thought, people misused words like dreadful; if they knew what dread was!—"but he's got a kind of weight, only he dissipates it. He undermines his mass. Don't you think so, Pauline?"

"I don't know," Pauline said shortly, and then added with private and lying malice: "I'm no judge of literature."

"Perhaps not," Adela said, "though I think it's more a question of general sensitiveness. Hugh, did you notice how the Parry talked of significance? Why, no one with a really *adult* mind could possibly—— O, good-bye, Pauline; I may see you to-morrow." Her voice passed away, accompanied by Hugh's temporary and lazy silence, and Pauline was left to Myrtle's monologues on the comforting friendliness of sunsets.

Even that had to stop when they reached the Foxes' hole. Myrtle, in a spasm of friendship for Messias, frequently called it that. As they parted upon the easy joke, Pauline felt the rest of the sentence pierce her. She took it to her with a sincerity of pain which almost excused the annexation—"the Son of Man hath not where to lay his head." It was the cry of her loneliness and fear, and it meant nothing to her mind but the empty streets and that fear itself. She went on.

# The Magus Zoroaster

Not to think; to think of something else. If she could. It was so hopeless. She was trying not to look ahead for fear she saw it, and also to look ahead for fear she was yielding to fear. She walked down the road quickly and firmly, remembering the many thousand times it had not come. But the visitation was increasing—growing nearer and clearer and more frequent. In her first twenty-four years she had seen it nine times; at first she had tried to speak of it. She had been told, when she was small, not to be silly and not to be naughty. Once, when she was adolescent, she had actually told her mother. Her mother was understanding in most things, and knew it. But at this the understanding had disappeared. Her eyes had become as sharp as when her husband, by breaking his arm, had spoiled a holiday in Spain which she—"for all their sakes" —had planned. She had refused to speak any more to Pauline that day, and neither of them had ever quite forgiven the other. But in those days the *comings*—as she still called them— had been rare; since her parents had died and she had been sent to live with and look after her grandmother in Battle Hill they had been more frequent, as if the Hill was fortunate and favourable to apparitions beyond men; a haunt of alien life. There had been nine in two years, as many as in all the years before. She could not speak of it to her grandmother, who was too old, nor to anyone else, since she had never discovered any closeness of friendship. But what would happen when the thing that was she came up to her, and spoke or touched? So far it had always turned aside, down some turning, or even apparently into some house; she might have been deceived were it not for the chill in her blood. But if some day it did not. . . .

A maid came out of a house a little farther down a road, and crossed the pavement to a pillar-box. Pauline, in the first glance, felt the sickness at her heart. Relieved, she reacted into the admission that she was only twenty-three houses away from her home. She knew every one of them; she had not avoided so much measurement of danger. It had never appeared to her indoors; not even on the Hill, which seemed to be so convenient for it. Sometimes she longed always to stay indoors; it could not be done, nor would she do it. She drove herself out, but the front door was still a goal and a protection. She always seemed to herself to crouch and cling before she left it, coveting the peace which everyone but she had . . . twenty-one, twenty. . . . She would *not* run; she would *not* keep her eyes on the pavement. She would walk steadily forward, head up and eyes before her . . . seventeen, sixteen. . . . She would think of something, of Peter Stanhope's play—"a terrible good". The whole world was for her a canvas printed with unreal figures, a curtain apt to roll up at any moment on one real figure. But this afternoon, under the stress of the verse, and then under the shock of Stanhope's energetic speech, she had fractionally wondered: a play—was there a play? a play even that was known by some? and then not without peace . . . ten, nine . . . the Magus Zoroaster; perhaps Zoroaster had not been frightened. Perhaps if any of the great—if Cæsar had met his own shape in Rome, or even Shelley . . . was there any tale of any who had? . . . six, five, four. . . .

Her heart sprang; there, a good way off—thanks to a merciful God—it was, materialized from nowhere in a moment. She knew it at once, however far, her own young figure, her own walk, her own dress and hat—had not her first sight of it been attracted so? changing, growing. . . . It was coming up at her pace—*doppelgänger*, *doppelgänger*: her control began to give . . . two . . . she didn't run, lest it should, nor did it. She reached her gate, slipped through, went up the path. If it should be running very fast up the road behind her now? She was biting back the scream and fumbling for her key. Quiet, quiet! "A terrible good." She got the key into the keyhole; she would not look back; would it click the gate or not? The door opened; and she was in, and the door banged behind her. She all but leant against it, only the *doppelgänger* might be leaning similarly on the other side. She went forward, her hand at her throat, up the stairs to her room, desiring (and with every atom of energy left denying that her desire could be vain) that there should be left to her still this one refuge in which she might find shelter.

## Chapter Two

# VIA MORTIS

Mrs. Parry and her immediate circle, among whom Adela Hunt was determinedly present, had come, during Pauline's private meditations, to several minor decisions, one of which was to ask Lawrence Wentworth to help with the costumes, especially the costumes of the Grand Ducal Court and Guard. Adela had said immediately that she would call on Mr. Wentworth at once, and Mrs. Parry, with a brief discontent, had agreed. While, therefore, Pauline was escaping from her ghostly twin, Adela and Hugh went pleasantly along other roads of the Hill to Wentworth's house.

It stood not very far from the Manor House, a little lower than that but still near to the rounded summit of the rise of ground which had given the place half its name. Lawrence Wentworth's tenancy was peculiarly suitable to the other half, for his intellectual concern was with the history of battle, and battles had continually broken over the Hill. Their reality had not been quite so neat as the diagrams into which he abstracted and geometricized them. The black lines and squares had swayed and shifted and been broken; the crimson curves, which had lain bloody under the moon, had been a mass of continuous tiny movement, a mass noisy with moans and screams. The Hill's chronicle of anguish had been due, in temporalities, to its strategic situation in regard to London, but a dreamer might have had nightmares of a magnetic attraction habitually there deflecting the life of man into death. It had epitomized the tale of the world. Prehistoric legends, repeated in early chronicles, told of massacres by

24

revolting Britons and roaming Saxons, mornings and evenings of hardly-human sport. Later, when permanent civilization arose, a medieval fortalice had been built, and a score of civil feuds and pretended loyalties had worn themselves out around it under kings who, though they were called Stephen or John, were as remote as Shalmanezer or Jeroboam. The Roses had twined there, their roots living on the blood shed by their thorns; the castle had gone up one night in fire, as did Rome, and the Manor House that followed had been raised in the midst of another order. A new kind of human civility entered; as consequence or cause of which, this Hill of skulls seemed to become either weary or fastidious. In the village that had stood at the bottom of the rise a peasant farmer, moved by some wandering gospeller, had, under Mary Tudor, grown obstinately metaphysical, and fire had been lit between houses and manor that he might depart through it in a roaring anguish of joy. Forty years later, under Elizabeth, the whispering informers had watched an outlaw, a Jesuit priest, take refuge in the manor, but when he was seized the Death of the Hill had sent him to its Type in London for more prolonged ceremonies of castration, as if it, like the men of the Renascence, seemed to involve its brutal origin in complications of religion and art. The manor had been forfeited to the Crown, but granted again to another branch of the family, so that, through all human changes, the race of owners had still owned. This endured, when afterwards it was sold to richer men, and even when Peter Stanhope had bought it back the house of his poetry remained faintly touched by the dreadful ease that was given to it by the labour and starvation of the poor.

The whole rise of ground therefore lay like a cape, a rounded headland of earth, thrust into an ocean of death. Men, the lords of that small earth, dominated it. The folklore of skies and seasons belonged to it. But if the past still lives in its own present beside our present, then the momentary later inhabitants were surrounded by a greater universe. From other periods of its time other creatures could crawl out of death, and invisibly contemplate the houses and people of the rise. The amphibia of the past dwelt about, and sometimes crawled out on, the slope of this world, awaiting the hour when they should either retire to their own mists or more fully invade the place of the living.

There had been, while the workmen had been creating the houses of the new estate, an incident which renewed the habit of the Hill, as if that magnetism of death was quick to touch first the more unfortunate of mortals. The national margin of unemployment had been reduced by the new engagement of labourers, and from the work's point of view reduced, in one instance, unwisely. A certain unskilled assistant had been carelessly taken on; he was hungry, he was ill, he was clumsy and slow. His name no one troubled to know. He shambled among the rest, their humorous butt. He was used to that; all his life he had been the butt of the world, generally of an unkind world. He had been repeatedly flung into the gutter by the turn of a hand in New York or Paris, and had been always trying to scramble out of it again. He had lost his early habit of complaining, and it only added to his passive wretchedness that his wife kept hers. She made what money she could by charing, at the market price, with Christmas Day, St. Stephen, and such feasts deducted, and since she usually kept her jobs, she could reasonably enjoy her one luxury of nagging her husband because he lost his. His life seemed to him an endless gutter down which ran an endless voice. The clerk of the works and his foreman agreed that he was no good.

An accidental inspection by one of the directors decided his discharge. They were not unkind; they paid him, and gave him an extra shilling to get a bus some way back towards London. The clerk added another shilling and the foreman sixpence. They told him to go; he was, on the whole, a nuisance. He went; that night he returned.

26

## Via Mortis

He went, towards the buses a mile off, tramping blindly away through the lanes, coughing and sick. He saw before him the straight gutter, driven direct to London across the lanes and fields. At its long end was a miserable room that had a perpetual shrill voice.

He longed to avoid them, and as if the Hill bade him a placable farewell there came to him as he left it behind him a quiet thought. He could simply reject the room and its voice; he could simply stop walking down the gutter. A fancy of it had grown in him once or twice before. Then it had been a fancy of some difficult act; now the act had suddenly become simple.

Automatically eating a piece of bread that one of the men had given him, he sat down by the roadside, looking round him to find the easiest way to what had suddenly become a resolve. Soft and pitiless the country stretched away round him, unwilling that he should die. He considered. There were brooks; he knew it was impossible for him to hold himself down in them while he drowned. There were motors, cars, or buses; apart from his unwillingness to get other people into trouble, he feared lest he should be merely hurt or maimed. He wanted to get himself completely out of trouble. There were the half-finished buildings away behind him. A magical and ghostly finger touched his mind; in one of those buildings he remembered to have seen a rope. In a dim way, as he sat gnawing his bread, he felt that this was the last trouble he would give to his fellows. Their care this time would be as hasty and negligent as ever, but it would be final. If the rope were not there, he would find some other way, but he hoped for the best. He even believed in that best.

He got up, sometime in the early evening, and began to plod back. It was not far and he was not old. In covering the short distance he covered age also, toiling doubly through space and time. The Republic, of which he knew nothing, had betrayed him; all the nourishment that comes from friendship and common pain was as much forbidden to him as the poor nourishment of his body. The Republic had decided that it was better one man, or many men, should perish, than the people in the dangerous chance of helping those many. It had, as always, denied supernatural justice. He went on, in that public but unspectacular abandonment, and the sun went down on him.

Under the moon he came on the Hill to a place which might have been an overthrown rather than an arising city. The chaos of that revolution which the Republic naturally refuses had rolled over it, or some greater disaster, the Vesuvian terror of Pompeii, or an invisible lava of celestial anger, as that which smote Thebes, or the self-adoring Cities of the Plain. Unfinished walls, unfilled pits, roofless houses, gaping holes where doors and windows were to be or had been spread before him. His body was shaking, but he went on. Here and there a ladder stretched upward; here and there a brazier burned. An occasional footstep sounded. The cold moon lit up the skeletons of houses, and red fires flickered rarely among them. He paused for a moment at the edge of the town, but not in doubt, only to listen if a watchman were near. From mere physical stress he whimpered a little now and then, but he did not change his purpose, nor did the universe invite him to change. It accepted the choice; no more preventing him than it prevents a child playing with fire or a fool destroying his love. It has not our kindness or our decency; if it is good, its goodness is of another kind than ours. It allowed him, moving from shadow to shadow, cautious and rash, to approach the house where he remembered to have seen the rope. All the afternoon the rope had been visible to his eyes. He knew exactly where it was; and there indeed it was. He slunk in and touched it, shivering and senseless but for the simple sense of life. The air of that infected place suffered his inhalations and filled his lungs as he dragged the rope, gently and softly, towards the nearest ladder beyond.

# Via Mortis

The ladder frightened him, lest it should be too much boarded, or else, bone-white in the moon, should, while he climbed, expose his yet living body to those universals who would have him live. But it was open for him, and he crouched within the lower shell of a room, holding the rope, peering, listening, waiting for he did not guess what until it came. He thought once he heard hurrying feet at a distance, but they were going from him, and presently all was again quiet. The moonlight gently faded; the white rungs grew shadowy; a cloud passed over the sky, and all was obscured. The heavens were kind, and the moon did not, like the sun, wait for a divine sacrifice in order to be darkened. A man served it as well. He rose, and slipped to the foot of his ladder. He went softly up, as the Jesuit priest had gone up his those centuries earlier paying for a loftier cause by a longer catastrophe. He went up as if he mounted on the bones of his body built so carefully for this; he clambered through his skeleton to the place of his skull, and receded, as if almost in a corporeal ingression, to the place of propinquent death. He went up his skeleton, past the skeleton frames of the ground floor, of the first floor. At the second the poles of the scaffold stretched upward into the sky. The roof was not on, nor his life built up. He dragged himself dizzily on to the topmost landing, pulling the rope after him, and there his crouching mind stayed. The cloud passed from the moon; another was floating up. His flesh, in which only his spirit now lived, was aware of the light. He still hoped for his best; he lay still.

Presently he peered over. The world allowed him to be capable and efficient at last; no one had seen him. The long gutter of his process was now coiled up into the rope he held; the room with its voice was away in and looked on him from the silent moon. He breathed, and a cloud floated over it again. There was nothing more to happen; everything had already happened except for one trifle which would be over soon. He tiptoed to the scaffold pole on his right hand, uncoiling the rope as he went; he pulled and gently shook it. It was slender, but it seemed strong. He took one end of the rope, began to fasten it to the end of the pole, and suddenly hesitated. It was a long rope; suppose it were too long, so that when he jumped he fell to the ground and was not dead but broken. Then all those people who, more fortunate than he, had governed him and shoved him into his gutter, would come to him again—he could hear a footstep or two of theirs upon the ground now, and lay still while they sounded and ceased—they would come to him and mind him and turn him out again, down a miry path under a perpetual talking moon that knew no wane. This was his one chance, for ever and ever, of avoiding them. He knew he must not miss it.

He measured out the rope to twice the length of his outstretched arms, and when the ruined city was once more silent he peered over, letting that measured section run through his hands. The end dangled much more than his height from the ground, and at that he twisted and knotted the next yard or two around the pole, straining against it, tugging it, making certain it could not ease loose. The moon emerged as he finished, and in a panic he dragged up the loose end, and shrank back from the edge, well back, so that no watcher should see him from the road. There, lying flat on his empty belly, he began his penultimate activity. He knotted, as best he could, the end of the rope about his neck, with a great and clumsy, but effective, slip knot. He tried it again and again, more fearful than ever lest its failure, because of his own, should betray him back into a life which his frenzy felt as already ghostly. He felt that he could not bear that last betrayal, for he would never have courage to repeat this mighty act of decision. The dreadful universe perhaps would spare him that, if he were careful now. He was very careful.

As, exhausted by the necessary labour, he lay flat on that stage of the spectral ascent, amid the poles and unroofed walls, he did not consider any future but unfortunate accident or fortunate death. He was almost shut up in his moment, and his hope was only that the next moment might completely close him in. No dichotomy of flesh and spirit distressed or delighted him, nor did he know anything of the denial of that dichotomy by the creed of Christendom. The unity of that creed has proclaimed, against experience, against intelligence, that for the achievement of man's unity the body of his knowledge is to be raised; no other fairer stuff, no alien matter, but this— to be impregnated with holiness and transmuted by lovely passion perhaps, but still this. Scars and prints may disseminate splendour, but the body is to be the same, the very body of the very soul that are both names of the single man. This man was not even terrified by that future, for he did not think of it. He desired only the end of the gutter and of the voice; to go no farther, to hear no more, to be done. Presently he remembered that time was passing; he must be quick or they would catch him, on his platform or as he fell, and if he fell into the safety of their hands he would fall into his old utter insecurity. All he knew of the comfort of the world meant only more pain. He got awkwardly to his feet; he must be quick.

He was not very quick. Something that was he dragged at him, and as he crawled to the edge dragged more frantically at something still in him. He had supposed he had wanted to die, and only at the last even he discovered that he wanted also not to die. Unreasonably and implacably, he wanted not to die. But also he wanted not to live, and the two rejections blurred his brain and shook his body. He half struggled to his feet in his agony; he twisted round and hung half over, his back to the abyss; he clutched at the rope, meaning to hold it and release it as he fell, to such an extreme of indecision pretending decision did his distress drive him, and then as the circling movement of his body ended, twining the rope once more round his neck, he swayed and yelped and knew that he was lost, and fell.

He fell, and as he fell he thought for a moment he saw below him a stir as of an infinite crowd, or perhaps, so sudden and universal was it, the swift rush of a million insects towards shelter, away from the shock that was he. The movement, in the crowd, in the insects, in the earth itself, passed outward towards the unfinished houses, the gaps and holes in half-built walls, and escaped. When at last he knew in his dazed mind that he was standing securely on the ground, he knew also, under the pale light which feebly shone over the unfashioned town, that he was still alone.

He stood for a moment in extreme fear that something would break out upon him from its hiding-place, but nothing moved, and as his fear subsided he was at leisure to begin to wonder what he had to do there. He recognized the place; it was the scene of his last job, the job from which he had been dismissed, the place to which, for a reason, he had returned. The reason? He looked round; all was quite still. There were no footsteps; there were no braziers, such as he had half expected, for he had thought a watch was set at night. There was no moon in the sky; perhaps it was not night. Indeed it was too light for night; perhaps it was dawn, but there was not yet a sun. As he thought of dawn and another day, he remembered why he was there. He had come there to die, and the rope was on the platform above. He did not quite understand why he was standing at the foot of the ladder, for he seemed to remember that he had mounted it, up to his head, unless he had jumped down to frighten something that had vanished, but it did not matter. What mattered was that dawn was here, and his time was short. Unless he acted, his chance and he would be lost. He went again, very quickly and anxiously, up the ladder. At the top he got on to the platform and hurried to find the rope. He had had it ready; he must not waste it. He looked round for it. The rope was not there.

At first he did not believe. This was certainly the place, though in the dawn which was less bright than the moon, and he knew he had hated the moon because it watched him, the corners of that stage between earth and sky were now in darkness. But he went and peered into them and felt. Uselessly. He knelt down, staring round, unaware of any sickness or exhaustion, only of anxiety. He almost lay down, screwing up his eyes, dragging himself round. It was all useless. The rope was not there.

By now, as he raised his head and looked out, the silence was beginning to trouble him, and the pallid dawn. It was good that the light should not grow, but also it was terrifying. There had not been much time, or had there? He could not attend to it; the absence of the rope preoccupied him. Could someone, out of the world that was filled with his rich enemies, have come, while he was down at the foot, doing something he could not remember, and run up the ladder quietly, and stolen back his rope as he himself had stolen it? Perhaps the men who had sent him off that day, or even his wife, out of the room, stretching a lean hand and snatching it, as she had snatched things before—but then she would have snarled or shrilled at him; she always did. He forgot his caution. He rose to his feet, and ran round and round seeking for it. He failed again; the rope was not there.

By the ladder he stood still, holding on to it, utterly defeated at last, in a despair that even he had never felt before. There had always been present to him, unrecognized but secure, man's last hope, the possibility of death. It may be refused, but the refusal, even the unrecognized refusal, admits hope. Without the knowledge of his capacity of death, however much he fear it, man is desolate. This had gone; he had no chance whatever. The rope was gone; he could not die. He did not yet know that it was because he was already dead.

The dead man stood there, a vast dead silence about him and within him. He turned his head this way and that. He no longer minded whether anyone came, and no one did come. He looked back over his shoulder at his platform and its dark corners. Some things were yet concealed. There was shadow; his eyes looked at it for a long while, some days or weeks, without interest or intelligence. Presently there was a stir in it, that presently ceased. He had been looking at it all that time, over his shoulder, still standing there and holding his ladder; his body, or what seemed to him to be his body, his whole consciousness of distances and shapes that seemed not to be he, slowly conforming itself to its intelligence of this other world. The silence of the dead was about him, the light of the dead was over him. He did not like the corners of darkness or the stir in the corners, and presently as he stood there he began to feel that he could get away from them. He knew now that he would not find the rope, that he would not take again the means he had once taken to escape from pain and fear, but in that utter quiet his despair began to discover itself to be more like contentment. He slid on to the ladder, vaguely determined to get as far as he could from the platform of transition. He went soundlessly down, and as he came to ground and loosed his hold he sighed; he took a step or two away and sighed again, and now for pure relief. He felt, through all his new world, the absence of men, the mere absence therefore of evil. The world which was to be represented, there, by the grand culture of Battle Hill, could offer him, after his whole life, no better thing than that it should keep away. Justice, so far, rescued him; what more there was had not yet begun to work. He wandered away over the Hill.

## Chapter Three

## QUEST OF HELL

It was in the house of the suicide that Lawrence Wentworth now sat. The dead man's corpse, discovered hanging in the morning, had been hugger-mugger interred, the body that then existed being then buried. With such bodies of past time the estate had no concern except to be silent about them, which it very successfully was. Wentworth, when he took the house, heard nothing of the most unfortunate incident, nor had any idea of what had happened in the space which now, properly closed and ceilinged, he had taken for his bedroom, any more than he saw through the window of his study the dead man occasionally return to the foot of the ladder which, in his world, still reached from earth to scaffolding. Neither of them was aware of the other.

Wentworth had at least one advantage over many other military historians; he had known war. He had served with some distinction, partly from luck, and partly from his brain which organized well. He had held a minor position on an army staff, and he had been alert at moving masses of men about and fitting them in, and removing them again. He could not win battles, but he could devise occupation for armies. He could always, when necessary, find somewhere for them to go and something for them to do, and he could deal with any objections to their going or doing that were raised. His mind reduced the world to diagrams, and he saw to it that the diagrams fitted. And as some such capacity is half of all ordinary leadership in war, he really had an insight into the technical side of the great military campaigns of the past. He could see what Cæsar or Napoleon had done, and why, and,

35

how; it was not to be expected that he could have seen it, as they did, before it happened. He had never had a friend or a lover; he had never, in any possible sense of the word, been "in love".

Yet, or perhaps therefore, his life had been pleasant to him, partly by the Fortune which confirms or ruins the care of generals, partly through his own instinctive tactical care. Only of late, especially since he had come to the Hill, the pleasantness had seemed to waver. He was not much over fifty, but his body was beginning to feel that its future was shortening, and that it had perhaps been too cautious in the past. His large opaque eyes, set widely in a squarish face, were acquiring a new restlessness. Also he had begun to dream. Something moved more sharply in his sleep, as the apparition of Pauline's terror moved more surely in the streets; the invisible life of the Hill quickening its pressure upon mental awareness.

It was a little dream, of no significance, as Mrs. Parry would have said; it was only a particular development of a common dream-thing, the state of something going on. He had no reason for disliking it except that it recurred. It was not complex; it was remarkably simple—simple and remarkable. He was climbing down a rope; he did nothing but climb down a rope. It was a white rope, so white that it shone of its own clarity in the pitch-black darkness where it and he existed, and it stretched up high above him, infinitely high, so that as he looked he could not see where or to what it was fastened. But that it was fastened both above and below was clear, for it was taut in his hands and between his legs, twisted expertly round it. He was not sliding down it; he was descending by the aid of knots which, though he could feel them against his hands and legs, he could never actually see in the rope as it emerged from his hands past his eyes. The descent was perplexing, for he never felt himself move and yet he knew he was continually farther down, down towards the bottom of·

the rope, the point and the place where it was secured beneath him. Once or twice he looked down and saw only the twined white strands stretching away in the black abyss. He felt no fear; he climbed, if he climbed, securely, and all the infinite black void did not terrify him; he would not fall. Nor did he fear the end—not *fear*; no monstrosity awaited him. On the other hand, he did, waking, remember to have felt the very slightest distaste, as if for a dentist. He remembered that he wanted to remain on the rope, but though he saw neither top nor bottom he was sure, in the dream, that that was impossible. A million yards or years of rope stretched above him; there might be a million years or yards below him. Or a hundred, or a score, or indeed but two or three. He climbed down, or else the rope climbed up, and about them was everlasting silence and the black night in which he and the rope only were visible, and only visible to himself.

It was mildly disagreeable; the more, and perhaps, if he had thought about it, only, because dreams, though negligible on waking, are so entirely ineluctable in sleep. Sleep had, all his life, been a pleasant thing to Wentworth; he had made of it an art. He had used himself to a composure that had readily accommodated itself to him. He made it a rule to think of pleasant things as he stretched himself in bed: his acquaintances sometimes, or the reviews—most of the reviews—of his last book, or his financial security, or his intentions about his immediate future work, or the permanent alterations he hoped he had caused in universal thought concerning Cæsar's employment of Balearic slingers during the campaigns in Gaul. Also, deliciously, his fancies would widen and change, and Cæsar would be drawing out cheques to pay his London Library subscriptions, or the Balearic slingers would be listening to him as he told them how they used to use their slings, and the next thing he would know would be either his housekeeper tapping at the door, or the light of morning, or, sometimes, the dream.

For this assault in sleep there were at least two personal reasons in his waking life, besides the nature of the Hill or the haunter of his house; one of them very much in the forefront of his mind, the other secret and not much admitted. The first was Aston Moffatt; the second was Adela Hunt. Aston Moffatt was another military historian, perhaps the only other worth mentioning, and Wentworth and he were engaged in a long and complicated controversy on the problem of the least of those skirmishes of the Roses which had been fought upon the Hill. The question itself was unimportant; it would never seriously matter to anyone but the controversialists whether Edward Plantagenet's cavalry had come across the river with the dawn or over the meadows by the church at about noon. But a phrase, a doubt, a contradiction, had involved the two in argument. Aston Moffatt, who was by now almost seventy, derived a great deal of intellectual joy from expounding his point of view. He was a pure scholar, a holy and beautiful soul who would have sacrificed reputation, income, and life, if necessary, for the discovery of one fact about the horse-boys of Edward Plantagenet. He had determined his nature. Wentworth was younger and at a more critical point, at that moment when a man's real concern begins to separate itself from his pretended, and almost to become independent of himself. He raged secretly as he wrote his letters and drew up his evidence; he identified scholarship with himself, and asserted himself under the disguise of a defence of scholarship. He refused to admit that the exact detail of Edward's march was not, in fact, worth to him the cost of a single cigar.

As for Adela, he was very well aware of Adela, as he was aware of cigars, but he did not yet know what he would give up for her, or rather for the manner of life which included her. As Aston Moffatt was bound either to lessen or heighten Wentworth's awareness of his own reputation, so Adela was bound either to increase or abolish his awareness of his age.

He knew time was beginning to hurry; he could at moments almost hear it scamper. He did not very well know what he wanted to do about it.

He was sitting now in his study, his large body leaning forward over the table, and his hands had paused in measuring the plan that lay in front of him. He was finding the answer to Aston Moffatt's last published letter difficult, yet he was determined that Moffatt could not be right. He was beginning to twist the intention of the sentences in his authorities, preferring strange meanings and awkward constructions, adjusting evidence, manipulating words. In defence of his conclusion he was willing to cheat in the evidence—a habit more usual to religious writers than to historical. But he was still innocent enough to be irritated; he felt, as it were, a roughness in the rope of his dream, and he was intensely awake to any other slights from any quarter. He looked sharply to see if there were more Moffatts in the world. At that inconvenient moment on that evening Adela arrived with Hugh. It was long since he had seen her in the company of one young man: alone, or with one woman, or with several young men and women, but not, as it happened, so. He stood up when they were announced, and as they came in, Adela's short red-and-cream thickness overshadowed by Hugh's rather flagrant masculinity, he felt something jerk in him, as if a knot had been first tied and then suddenly pulled loose. He had written but that morning in an article on the return of Edward IV, "the treachery of the Earl destroyed the balance". Remote, five hundred years away, he felt it in the room; a destruction of balance. Then they were sitting down and Adela was talking.

She explained, prettily, why they had come. Hugh, watching, decided that she must not behave quite so prettily. Hugh had no jerks or quavers. He had decided some time since that Adela should marry him when he was ready, and was giving himself the pleasurable trouble of making this clear to her. There was a touch too much gusto in her manner towards

Wentworth. She had been, as he had, and some others of the young, in the habit of spending an evening, once a fortnight or so, at Wentworth's house, talking about military history and the principles of art and the nature of the gods. During the summer these informal gatherings were less frequent, because of tennis and motor-rides and the nature of men and women. Hugh meant that for Adela they should stop altogether. He observed an intimacy; he chose that it should not continue, partly because he wished Adela to belong to him and partly because the mere action of breaking it would show how far Adela was prepared to go with him. His mind made arrangements.

Adela explained. Wentworth said: "Very well, I'll do anything I can. What is it you want?" He felt ungracious; he blamed Aston Moffatt.

"O, the costumes," Adela answered. "The Guard especially. The Grand Duke has a guard, you see, though there didn't seem to be much point in it. But it has a fight with the robbers, and if you'd see that it fought reasonably well. . . ." She did not trouble to enlarge on her own view that the fight ought to be quite unrealistic; she knew that Mr. Wentworth did not much care for non-realistic art, and till recently she had preferred her mild satisfaction with her invasion of Wentworth's consciousness to any bigotry of artistic interpretation.

Hugh said: "It'd be frightfully good of you to give me a hand with my Guard, Mr. Wentworth." He infused the "Mister" with an air of courteous deference to age, and as he ended the sentence he stretched and bent an arm in the lazy good humour of youth. Neither of the others analysed stress and motion, yet their blood was stirred, Adela faintly flushing with a new gratification, Wentworth faintly flushing with a new anger. He said, "Are you to be the Grand Duke then, Prescott?"

"So Mrs. Parry seems to suggest," Hugh answered, and added, as if a thought had struck him, "unless—Adela, d'you think Mr. Wentworth would take the part himself? Isn't that an idea?"

Before Adela could answer Wentworth said: "Nonsense; I've never acted in my life."

"I'm quite sure," Hugh said, leaning comfortably forward with his elbows on his knees and his strong hands interlocked, "that you'd be a better father for the princess than I should. I think there's no doubt Adela'll have to be the princess."

"O, I don't see that," said Adela, "though it's true Mrs. Parry . . . but there are lots of others. But, Mr. Wentworth, would you? You'd give it a kind of . . ." she thought of "age" and substituted "force". "I was saying to Hugh as we came along that all it needs is force."

"I certainly wouldn't take it away from Prescott," Wentworth said. "He's much better at these games than I could be." He had tried to give to the words a genial and mature tolerance, but he heard them as merely hostile; so did the others.

"Ah, but then," Hugh answered, "you know such a lot about battles and history—battles long ago. You'd certainly be more suitable for Adela's father—sir."

Wentworth said: "I'll keep myself for the Guard. What period did you say?"

"They seem to think 1700," Adela said. "I know Mrs. Parry said something about eighteenth-century uniforms. She's going to write to you."

Hugh stood up. "So we oughtn't to keep you," he added. "Adela and I are going back to talk to her now. Come on, duchess—or whatever it is they call you."

Adela obeyed. Wentworth noted, with an interior irritation, that she really did. She moved to rise with something more than consent. It was what he had never had—consent, yes, but not this obedience. Hugh had given her his hand to pull her up, and in that strained air the movement was a proclamation. He added, as she stood by his side: "Do change

your mind, sir, and show us all how to be a *Grand Siècle* father.
I'll ask Mrs. Parry to put it to you."

"You certainly won't," Wentworth said. "I've no time to
be a father."

"Odd way of putting it," Hugh said when they were outside.
"I don't know why your Mr. Wentworth should be so peeved
at the idea. Personally, I rather like it."

Adela was silent. She was well aware of the defiance—nor
even a defiance, the rumour of a struggle long ago—that
Hugh had brought into the conversation. Wentworth had been
relegated, for those few sentences, to his place in the shadowy
past of Battle Hill. The notice he had taken of her had been
a dim flattery; now it was more dim and less flattering. She
had been increasingly aware, since she had met Hugh, of her
militant blood; of contemporary raid and real contest, as of
some battle "where they charge on heaps the enemy flying".
But she did not quite wish to lose Lawrence Wentworth; he
had given her books, he had friends in London, he could
perhaps be useful. She desired a career. She could be sensationally deferential on Thursday, if, as she expected, she went
to him on Thursday. There had been, at the last gathering,
ten days before, an agreement on next Thursday. She had
just accomplished this decision when Hugh said: "By the
way, I wanted to ask you something. What about next
Thursday?"

"Next Thursday?" she said, startled.

"Couldn't you come out somewhere in the evening?"

"But . . ." Adela paused, and Hugh went on: "I thought
we might have dinner in town, and go to a show if you
liked."

"I'd love it," Adela said. "But it needn't be Thursday?"

"I'm afraid it must," Hugh answered. "There's tennis at
the Foxes' on Monday, and Tuesday and Wednesday I shall
be late at work, and Friday we're to read the play, and the
Parry's almost certain to want us on the Saturday too."

Adela said again: "I'd love it, but I was going to Mr. Wentworth's on Thursday. I mean, we've been going rather steadily, and last time I practically promised."

"I know you did," said Hugh. "So did I, but we can't help it."

"Couldn't we go another week?" Adela asked.

"With this play about?" Hugh said sardonically. "My dear, we're going to be clutched by rehearsals every evening. Of course, we can leave it if you'd rather, but you said you'd like to see that thing *The Second Pylon*—it's your style—and as it's only on till Saturday . . . well, as a matter of fact, I got a couple of tickets for Thursday on the chance. I knew it'd be our only night."

"Hugh!" Adela exclaimed. "But I want frightfully to see it; they say it's got the most marvellous example of this Surrealist plastic cohesion. O, Hugh, how splendid of you! The only thing is. . . ."

"Pauline'll be going to Wentworth's, won't she?" Hugh said. "And probably others. He can talk to them."

They were both aware that this would be by no means the same thing. They were equally both aware that it was what was about to happen; and that by Thursday evening it would have happened. Adela found that her hesitation about the future had already become a regret for the past: the thing had been done. A willing Calvinist, she said: "I hope he won't think it rude. He's been very nice."

"Naturally," Hugh answered. "But now it's up to you to be nice. Grand Dukes ought to be gratified, oughtn't they?"

"You asked him to be the Grand Duke," Adela pointed out.

"I asked him to be your father," Hugh said. "I don't think I had any notion of his being a Grand Duke."

He looked at her, laughing. "Write him a note on Wednesday," he said, "and I'll ring him up on Thursday evening from London, and ask him to make my excuses to you and **Pauline and the rest.**"

"Hugh!" Adela exclaimed, "you couldn't!" Then, dimpling and gurgling, she added: "He's been very kind to me. I should hate him to feel hurt."

"So should I," Hugh said gravely. "Very well; that's settled."

Unfortunately for this delicate workmanship, the two or three other young creatures who had shared, with Adela, Hugh, and Pauline, the coffee and culture of Wentworth's house, were also deflected from it on that Thursday by tennis or the play; unfortunately, because the incidents of the Saturday had left him more acutely conscious at once of his need for Adela and of his need for flattery. He did not fully admit either; he rather defended himself mentally against Hugh's offensiveness that surrendered to his knowledge of his desire. Even so he refused to admit that he was engaged in a battle. He demanded at once security and victory, a habit not common to those great masters whose campaigns he studied. He remembered the past—the few intimate talks with Adela, the lingering hands, the exchanged eyes. Rather like Pompey, he refused to take measures against the threat on the other side the Rubicon; he faintly admitted that there was a Rubicon, but certainly not that there might be a Cæsar. He assumed that the Rome which had, he thought, admired him so much and so long, was still his, and he desired it to make his ownership clear. He was prepared to overlook that Saturday as not being Adela's fault as soon as the Thursday should bring him Adela's accustomed propinquity; perhaps, for compensation's sake and for promise of a veiled conclusion, a little more than propinquity. It was the more shattering for him that her note only reached him by the late post an hour or so before his guests usually arrived.

She had had, she said, to go to town that day to see about the stuff for her costume; things would be rushed, and she hadn't liked to make difficulties. She was dreadfully distressed; she might well be, he thought, with a greater flush of anger

44

than he knew. He glanced at another note of excuse almost with indifference. But he was still ruffled when Pauline arrived, and it was with a certain abruptness that he told her he expected no one else but Prescott.

When, ten minutes later, the telephone bell rang, and he heard Prescott's voice offering his own regrets and explaining that absolutely unavoidable work kept him at the office: would Mr. Wentworth be so good as to apologize to Adela?—he was not sure if he were glad or sorry. It saved him from Prescott, but it left him tiresomely alone with Pauline. Pauline had a recurrent tendency to lose the finer point of military strategy in an unnecessary discussion of the sufferings of the rank and file; neither of them knew that it was the comfort of his house and his chairs—not to reckon her companionship with men in grief—which incited her. He did not think he wanted to have to talk to Pauline, but he was pleased to think he need not carry Hugh's message to Adela. He could not, of course, know that Adela was then squeezed into the same telephone box as Hugh. She had objected at first, but Hugh had pleasantly overpersuaded her, and it was true she did want to know exactly what he said—so as to know. And it was attractive to hear him telephone apologies to her when she was close at his side, to listen to the cool formality with which he dispatched ambassadorial messages to phantom ears, so that her actual ears received the chill while her actual eyes sparkled and kindled at his as he stood with the receiver at his ear. He said—as Wentworth only realized when he had put down his own receiver—"and would you be kind enough to make my apologies to Adela?" She mouthed "and the others" at him, but he shook his head ever so little, and when, as he put back the receiver, she said, "But you ought to have sent your message to Pauline at least," he answered, "Wentworth'll see to that; I wasn't going to mix you up." She said, "But supposing he doesn't, it'll look so rude," expecting him to answer that he didn't care. Instead of which, as they emerged

45

from the call-box, he said, "Wentworth'll see to it; he won't like not to." She sat down to dinner infinitely more his accomplice than she had been when she had met him first that evening.

In effect he was right. Wentworth had received a slight shock when the single name reached his ears, but it was only on his way back to the study that he realized that he was being invited to assist Prescott's approach towards Adela. He must, of course, enlarge the apology, especially since Adela anyhow wasn't there, as he hadn't troubled to explain. Prescott could find that out for himself. Since he didn't know —a throb of new suspicion held him rigid outside his study door. It was incredible, because Prescott wouldn't have sent the message, or any message, if he and Adela had been together. But they were both away, and that (his startled nerves reported to his brain) meant that they were together. His brain properly reminded him that it meant nothing of the sort. But of that saving intelligence his now vibrating nervous system took no notice whatever. It had never had a chance to disseminate anarchy before, and now it took its chance. Fifty years of security dissolved before one minute of invasion; Cæsar was over the Rubicon and Pompey was flying from Rome. Wentworth strode back into the study and looked at Pauline much as Pompey might have looked at a peculiarly unattractive senator.

He said: "Prescott can't come either. He sends you his apologies," and with an extreme impatience waited to hear whether she had any comment to make upon this, which might show what and how much, if anything, she knew. She only said, "I'm sorry. Is he working late?"

It was exactly what Wentworth wanted to know. He went back to his usual seat at the corner of his large table, and put down his cigar. He said, "So he says. It's unfortunate, isn't it, just the evening Adela couldn't come?" He then found himself pausing, and added, "But we can go on talking, can't we? Though I'm afraid it will be duller for you."

He hoped she would deny this at once; on the other hand he didn't want her to stop. He wanted her to want to stop, but to be compelled to go by some necessary event; so that her longing and disappointment could partly compensate him for Adela's apparently volitional absence, but without forcing him to talk. He wished her grandmother could be taken worse suddenly. But she made no sign of going, nor did she offer him any vivid tribute. She sat for a minute with her eyes on the floor, then she looked at him and said: "There was something I thought of asking you."

"Yes?" Wentworth said. After all, Prescott probably was at his office, and Adela probably—wherever she had to be.

Pauline had not formally intended to speak. But Lawrence Wentworth was the only person she knew who might be aware of . . . what these things were and what they demanded. And since they were thus left together, she consented to come so far as to ask. She disdained herself a little, but she went on, her disdain almost audible in her voice: "Did you ever come across"—she found she had to pause to draw equable breath; it was difficult even to hint—"did you ever read of any tale of people meeting themselves?"

Momentarily distracted, Wentworth said: "Meeting themselves? What, in dreams?"

"Not dreams," Pauline said, "meeting themselves . . . in the street . . . or anywhere." She wished now she hadn't begun, for to speak seemed to invite its presence, as if it were likely to hover outside, if not inside the house; and she would have to go home by herself to-night the whole way. . . . Or, since she had betrayed its privacy, supposing it followed up her betrayal and came now. . . .

"There's a picture of Rossetti's," Wentworth said; "were you thinking of that?"

"Not a picture," Pauline said; "I mean, have you ever read of its happening? Shelley says it happened to Zoroaster."

"Indeed," Wentworth said. "I don't remember that. Of

47

course I've heard of it as a superstition. Where have you come across it? Has anyone you know been seeing themselves?"

His mind was drifting back to Adela; the question rang hard. Pauline felt the obstruction and stayed. She said, "I knew a girl who thought she did. But don't let me bother you."

"You aren't bothering me," Wentworth said by force of habit. "On the contrary. I never remember to have come across anything of the sort, though I've a notion it was supposed to foretell death. But then almost any unusual incident is supposed to foretell death by the savage—or let's say the uncivilized—mind. Death, you see, is inevitably the most unusual incident, and so—by correspondence—the lesser is related to the greater. Anthropology is very instructive in that way. The uneducated mind is generally known by its haste to see likeness where no likeness exists. It evaluates its emotions in terms of fortuitous circumstance. It objectifies its concerns through its imagination. Probably your friend was a very self-centred individual."

Pauline said coldly, "I don't know that she was," while Wentworth wondered if Adela and Prescott had finished the supper they were not, of course, having together. Their absence was a fortuitous circumstance. He evaluated his emotions in its terms, and (like any barbarian chief) objectified his concerns by his imagination. She could find out the difference between Prescott and himself. But he didn't mind; he didn't mind. He curvetted on that particular horse for a while, and while curvetting he took no notice of Pauline's remark until the silence startled his steed into nearly throwing him. Still just remaining seated, he said, "O, she isn't, isn't she?" and thought how lank, compared to Adela, Pauline was—lank and blank. She had no capacity. Exactly what capacity she lacked he did not carefully consider, assuming it to be intellectual: the look, not the eyes; the gesture, not the hand. It was Adela's mental alertness which he knew he would have grudged Prescott, if he could grudge anybody anything. This conversation about people seeing themselves was the dullest he had ever known; he looked covertly at the clock on the mantelpiece; at the same moment Pauline, also covertly, looked at her wrist-watch. She had been a fool to say anything; the only result was to expose her more consciously to that other approach. She had better get home, somehow, before she did anything sillier. She said, "Thank you", and couldn't think of anything else. She got up therefore, and said the only thing left.

"My grandmother's not been so well to-day. Would you forgive me if I deserted you too? We're treating you shockingly, aren't we?"

Wentworth got up alertly. "Not a bit," he said. "I'm sorry. I'm sorry you feel you ought to go." It occurred to him that, later on, he might walk down toward the station. If he met them together, he would at least be justified. They might have met at Marylebone, of course, even if he did meet them; and if he didn't, they might be coming by a later train. He might wait for the next. Perhaps it would be wiser not to go— he couldn't, in his position, hang about for ever and ever. People chattered. But he would decide about that when this superfluous being had been dismissed. He went with her to the door, was genial and bright, said good night, snarled at the time she took getting to the gate, and at last was free to make up his mind.

He could not do it. He was driven by his hunger as the dead man who had come to that unbuilt house had been driven by his, and for some time he wandered about his rooms as that other shape had gone through the streets, seeking peace and finding none. At last he found himself in his bedroom, looking out of the window, as the dead man had stood there looking over the ruins of history, from the place of his skull. Wentworth stood there now for some seconds, exercising a no more conscious but a still more deliberate choice. He also yielded—to the chaos within rather than the chaos without.

The dead man had had reason to suppose that to throw himself down would mean freedom from tyranny, but Wentworth was not so much of a fool as to think that to thrust himself into the way of possible discovery would mean any such freedom. A remnant of intelligence cried to him that this was the road of mania, and self-indulgence leading to mania. Self-preservation itself urged him to remain; lucidity urged him, if not love. He stood and looked and listened, as the dead man had looked and listened. He heard faint hurrying footsteps somewhere on the Hill; the moon was covered by a cloud. The shadow provoked him; in it they might be, now, passing the end of his road. He must act before it was too late. He would not go to spy; he would go for a walk. He went out of the room, down the soft swift stairs of his mind, into the streets of his mind, to find the phantoms of his mind. He desired hell.

He strode out on his evening walk. He walked down the length of his road; if that led towards the station it could not be helped, nor if at a point it joined the road which Adela would take from the station. He was a man, and he had a right to his walk. He was not a child, neither the child that had lost its toy and cried for it, nor the child that had lost its toy and would not let itself care, nor the child that had lost its toy and tried to recover it by pretending it never did care. It may be a movement towards becoming like little children to admit that we are generally nothing else. But he was; he was a man, he was going for his walk.

At the junction of roads, as at a junction of his mind, he stopped and waited—to enjoy the night air. His enjoyment strained intently and viciously to hear the sounds of the night, or such as were not of too remote and piercing a quality to reach him. The wind among the hills was fresh. He heard at a distance a train come in, and the whistle of its departure. One or two travellers went by; one, a woman, hurrying, said something to him as she passed—good night or good morning; it sounded, in his strained joy, like both. He became aware that he was visible in the moon; he moved back into shadow. If he saw them coming he could walk away or walk on without seeming to be in ambush. He was not in ambush; he was out for a walk.

An hour and more went by. He walked back, and returned. His physical nature, which sometimes by its mere exhaustion postpones our more complete damnation, did not save him. He was not overtired by his vigil, nor in that extreme weariness was the vision of a hopeless honour renewed. He paced and repaced, cannibal of his heart. Midnight passed; the great tower clock struck one. He heard the last train come in. A little up the road, concealed in the shadow, he waited. He heard the light patter of quick feet; he saw, again, a woman go hurrying by. He thought for a moment she was Adela, and then knew she was not. Other feet came, slower and double. The moon was bright; he stood at the edge of his own skull's platform; desire to hate and desire not to hate struggled in him. In the moonlight, visible, audible, arm in arm, talking and laughing, they came. He saw them pass; his eyes grew blind. Presently he turned and went home. That night when at last he slept he dreamed, more clearly than ever before, of his steady descent of the moon-bright rope.

## Chapter Four

# VISION OF DEATH

Pauline's parents had both died a few years before, and she had been put in Battle Hill to live with her grandmother for two reasons. The first was that she had no money. The second was that her uncle refused "to leave his mother to strangers". Since Pauline's mother had never liked her husband's parents, the girl had practically never seen the old lady. But the blood relationship, in her uncle's mind, connoted intimacy, and he found an occupation for an orphan and a companion for a widow at one stroke of mercy. Pauline was furious at the decisive kindness which regulated her life, but she had not, at the time when it interfered, found a job, and she had been so involved with the getting to Battle Hill that she discovered herself left there, at last, with her grandmother, a nurse, and a maid. Even so, it was the latent fear in her life that paralysed initiative; she could respond but she could not act. Since they had been on the Hill and the visitations had grown more frequent, she felt that deep paralysis increasing, and she kept her hold on social things almost desperately tight. Her alternative was to stop in altogether, to bury herself in the house, and even so to endure, day by day, the fear that her twin might resolve out of the air somewhere in the hall or the corridor outside her own room. She hated to go out, but she hated still more to stop in, and her intelligence told her that the alternative might save her nothing in the end. Rigid and high-headed she fled, with a subdued fury of pace, from house to gathering, and back from gathering to house, and waited for her grandmother to die.

# Vision of Death

Her grandmother, ignoring the possible needs of the young, went on living, keeping her room in the morning, coming down to lunch, and after a light early dinner retiring again to her room. She made no great demands on her granddaughter, towards whom indeed she showed a delicate social courtesy; and Pauline in turn, though in a harsher manner, maintained towards her a steady deference and patience. The girl was in fact so patient with the old lady that she had not yet noticed that she was never given an opportunity to be patient. She endured her own nature and supposed it to be the burden of another's.

On an afternoon in early June they were both in the garden at the back of the house; the walls that shut it in made it a part of the girl's security. Pauline was learning her part, turning the typescript on her knees, and shaping the words with silent lips. The trouble about some of them was that they were so simple as to be almost bathos. Her fibres told her that they were not bathos, until she tried to say them, and then, it was no good denying, they sounded flat. She put the stress here and there; she tried slowness and speed. She invoked her conscious love to vocalize her natural passion, and the lines made the effort ridiculous. She grew hot as she heard herself say them, even though she did not say them aloud. Her unheard melody was less sweet than her memory of Stanhope's heard, but she did not then think of him reading, only of the lines he had read. They were simple with him; with her they were pretentious and therefore defiled.

She looked up at Mrs. Anstruther, who was sitting with her eyes closed, and her hands in her lap. Small, thin, wrinkled, she was almost an ideal phenomenon of old age. Some caller, a day or two before, had murmured to Pauline on leaving: "She's very fragile, isn't she?" Pauline, gazing, thought that fragile was precisely not the word. Quiet, gentle, but hardly passive and certainly not fragile. Even now, on that still afternoon, the shut eyes left the face with a sense of preoccupation

53

—translucent rock. She was absent, not with the senility of a spirit wandering in feeble memories, but with the attention of a worker engrossed. Perhaps Stanhope looked so when he wrote verse. Pauline felt that she had never seen her grandmother before and did not quite know what to make of her now. A light sound came from the garden beyond. Mrs. Anstruther opened her eyes and met Pauline's. She smiled. "My dear," she said, "I've been meaning to ask you something for the last day or two." Pauline thought it might be the hot afternoon that gave the voice that effect of distance; it was clear, but small and from afar. The words, the tone, were affectionate with an impersonal love. Pauline thought: "She might be talking to Phœbe"—Phœbe being the maid—and at the same time realized that Mrs. Anstruther did so talk to Phœbe, and to everyone. Her good will diffused itself in all directions. Her granddaughter lay in its way, with all things besides, and it mingled with the warm sun in a general benediction.

Pauline said: "Yes, grandmother?"

"If by any chance I should die during the next few weeks," Mrs. Anstruther said, "you won't let it interfere with your taking part in the play, will you? It would be so unnecessary."

Pauline began to speak, and hesitated. She had been on the point of beginning formally: "O, but——" when she felt, under the lucid gaze, compelled to intelligence. She said slowly: "Well, I suppose I should have. . . ."

"Quite unnecessary," Mrs. Anstruther went on, "and obviously inconvenient, especially if it were in the last few days. Or the last. I hoped you wouldn't think of it, but it was better to make sure."

"It'll look very odd," said Pauline, and found herself smiling back. "And what will the rest of them think?"

"One of them will be disappointed; the rest will be shocked but relieved," Mrs. Anstruther murmured. "You've no proper understudy?"

"None of us have," Pauline said. "One of the others in the Chorus would have to take my part . . . if I were ill, I mean."

"Do any of them speak verse better than you?" Mrs. Anstruther asked, with a mild truthfulness of inquiry.

Pauline considered the Chorus. "No," she said at last, sincerely. "I don't think . . . I'm sure they don't. Nor Adela," she added with a slight animosity against the princess. Her grandmother accepted the judgment. "Then it would be better for you to be there," she said. "So you'll promise me? It will very nearly be a relief."

"I'll promise certainly," Pauline said. "But you don't feel worse, do you, my dear? I thought you'd been stronger lately —since the summer came in."

" 'I have a journey, sir, shortly to go,' " Mrs. Anstruther quoted. "And a quieter starting-place than our ancestor."

"Our ancestor?" Pauline said, surprised. "O, but I remember. He was martyred wasn't he?"

Mrs. Anstruther quoted again: " 'Then the said Struther being come to the stake, cried out very loudly: *To him that hath shall be given*, and one of the friars that went with him struck at him and said: *Naughty heretic, and what of him that hath not?* and he shouted with a great laughter, pointing at the friar, and calling out: *He shall lose all that he hath*, and again *The Lord hath sent away the rich with empty bellies*. Then they stripped him, and when he was in his shirt he looked up and said: *The ends of the world be upon me*; and so they set him at the stake and put the fire to the wood, and as the fire got hold of him he gave a loud cry and said: *I have seen the salvation of my God*, and so many times till he died. Which was held for a testimony that the Lord had done great things for him there in the midst of the fire, and under the Lady Elizabeth the place was called Struther's Salvation for many years.' "

Mrs. Anstruther stopped. "And perhaps the Lord did," she said, "though I would not quite take Foxe's word for it."

Pauline shuddered. "It was a terrible thing," she said. "How he could shout for joy like that!"

"Salvation," Mrs. Anstruther said mildly, "is quite often a terrible thing—a frightening good."

"A . . ." said Pauline, and paused. "Mr. Stanhope said something like that," she ended.

"Peter Stanhope is a great poet," her grandmother answered. "But I don't think many of you can possibly understand his play. You may; I can't tell."

"Mrs. Parry·understands it, all but the Chorus," Pauline said. "And Adela and Myrtle Fox understand even that."

Mrs. Anstruther's look changed. She had been contemplating the fact of Stanhope's poetry with a gaze of awe; there entered into that awe a delicate and extreme delight. She said: "My dear, I used to know Catherine Parry very well. No one has destroyed more plays by successful production. I sometimes wonder—it's wrong—whether she has done the same thing with her life. It's wrong; she is a good creature, and she has behaved very well in all her unrehearsed effects. But I feel she relies too much on elocution and not enough on poetry."

Pauline meditated on this. "I don't think I quite understand," she said. "How the elocution?"

"You're a little inclined to it yourself, my dear," Mrs. Anstruther answered. "Your elocution is very just and very effective, but a certain breath of the verse is lacking. No one could have been kinder to me than you have. We've done very well together—I as the patient and you as the keeper. That's what I mean by elocution."

She turned on her granddaughter eyes full of delight and affection. Pauline could only sit and stare. Then slowly a blush crept up her face, and she looked hastily away.

"Ah, don't be distressed," the old woman said. "My dear, you've been perfect. You're in trouble over something, and yet you've always been kind. I wish I could have helped you."

"I'm not in any trouble," Pauline said with a slight harshness, "except now. Have I been stupid, grandmother?"

"That," Mrs. Anstruther said, "was perhaps a little less than intelligent. Why do you refuse to lean?"

"I don't," Pauline said bitterly, "but there's no——" She was on the point of saying "no help in leaning"; she recovered herself, and changed it to "no need to lean".

"O, my dear child," Mrs. Anstruther murmured gently, "that's almost like the speech days at my school. Ask Peter Stanhope to tell you how to read verse."

Confused between metaphor, implication, and rebuke, and the voice that disseminated sweetness through all, Pauline was about to protest again when Phœbe came out into the garden. She came up to her mistress, and said: "Mrs. Lily Sammile has called, madam, and wants to know if you are well enough to see her."

"Certainly," Mrs. Anstruther said. "Ask Mrs. Sammile to come out here." And as Phœbe disappeared: "Do you know her, Pauline?"

Pauline, standing up and folding her typescript with a precision that was almost respect, said: "Hardly *know*. She meets one continually, and she's at things. She calls. I never met anyone who'd called on her, now I come to think of it. I don't even know where she lives."

"There are all sorts of places to live on this hill," Mrs. Anstruther said, and Pauline heard in the voice an undertone of ambiguity. For a moment her fear took her; she looked hastily round. There was no sign of her twin. "All sorts of places to live."

"Many habitations," she answered with forced lightness, and went to meet the visitor who appeared from the house.

Mrs. Sammile was younger than Mrs. Anstruther, and much quicker in movement. She was much more restless. Her feet pattered on the path, her eyes glanced everywhere; she suggested by her whole bearing that time was in a hurry, and there was very little time for—something. Perhaps the contrast of Mrs. Anstruther's repose heightened this excitement. She was shorter than Pauline, and her eyes looked up at the girl almost anxiously. She said: "I've only just looked in. But it was so *long* since I'd seen you."

"We met yesterday, if you remember," Pauline answered, smiling. "But it was good of you to come."

"I don't, I hope, intrude?" Mrs. Sammile went on, as she shook hands with the old woman. Mrs. Anstruther murmured something vague, and Pauline said it more definitely: "Of course not, Mrs. Sammile, we're delighted."

"Such glorious weather—but trying, isn't it?" the visitor prattled nervously on, rather like a chicken fluttering round the glass walls of a snake's cage. "I always think any weather's trying, heat or cold. And it always seems to be one or other, doesn't it?"

"So pleasant," said Mrs. Anstruther politely. "Like sex, one can't imagine anything not one or the other. Or, of course, a combination."

"If," Pauline added, valiant but aware of failure, "if we could make our own weather. . . ."

Lily Sammile slewed round a little towards her. "If we *could!*" she said. "I thought yesterday that you were looking a little tired, my dear."

"Was I?" Pauline answered. "Perhaps I was," and added, agonizingly, "It's the spring, I expect."

The other looked at her, turning still a little more away from Mrs. Anstruther, and seeming to become a little quieter as she did so. She said: "I do think the world's rather trying, don't you?"

"I do," Pauline said with a heartfelt throb of assent, and more earnestly than she knew. "Very trying." It certainly was hot. She felt that three in the garden were too many, and wondered if her grandmother, in case she was feeling tired, ought to be offered an opportunity of going indoors. If June were so sultry, what would July be? The time was still; no sound came. A lifting palpitation took her; she shuddered. Her grave: who walked on, or was it from, her grave? The thing she had so often seen? into which—she knew now— she feared to be drawn, to be lost or not to be lost, to be always herself as the enfeebled element in something else. Never yet within walls, but the heat crept round her, a pre- liminary invasion; the heat came over or through walls, and after the heat its centre.

The violent sensation receded. She came to herself to find herself staring rudely at Mrs. Sammile's face. It was a face that had been beautiful, rounded and precious with delight, sustained just sufficiently by its bones to avoid, as for instance Adela Hunt's hardly avoided, the reproach of plumpness; and was still full in places, by the ears and round the jaw; only the cheeks were a little macabre in their withdrawal, and the eyes in their hint of hollows about them. Pauline, stirred by the sad recollection of her other self, thought that Mrs. Sammile looked more like death than her grandmother, more like a living death, than which, on this hill where her own ancestor and so many others had died, what could be more likely?

Mrs. Sammile was saying softly: "Perhaps she's asleep; I don't want to wake her. You look so tired. If I could be any use. . . ."

Pauline thought, as she looked back, that she had been un- just to Mrs. Sammile's eyes. They were not restless, as she had thought. They were soothing; they appealed and comforted at once. She said: "I've had bad dreams."

Mrs. Sammile said: "I've had them too, sometimes," and Pauline almost felt that even her dream, to call it that, was less trouble than those other undescribed nightmares. But before she could speak the visitor went on: "But there are cures, you know."

# Vision of Death

She had spoken, perhaps, a little more loudly, for Mrs. Anstruther's voice answered equably: "There is, of course, sleep. Or waking. Is there anything else?"

Mrs. Sammile looked round and her answer held the earlier suggestion of hostility. She said, defensively: "Pleasanter dreams. On a hill like this, one ought to have a choice. There are so many."

Pauline said: "Can you change dreams, Mrs. Sammile?"

"O, everyone can," the other answered. She leant towards Pauline and went on: "There are all sorts of ways of changing dreams." She put a hand on the girl's. "All tales of the brain. Why not tell yourself a comforting tale?"

"Because I could never make up a satisfying end," Pauline said, "and the tale wouldn't stop—no tale that I could think of. There was always something more that had got to happen and I could never feel—not in my best tale—that I was quite certainly telling it."

"You must let me tell you tales instead," Lily Sammile answered. "Come and see me."

"I'd like to, but I don't think I know where you live, Mrs. Sammile," Pauline said, and paused on the implied question.

Mrs. Sammile said: "O, we shall meet. And if we can't find a tale we'll do as well. Cross my hand with silver, and I'll not only tell you a good fortune, I'll make you one. Like the Bible—wine and milk without money, or for so little it hardly counts."

Pauline looked at Mrs. Anstruther. "Mrs. Sammile is offering us all we want without any trouble," she said. "Shall we take it and be grateful?"

"Exquisite rhetoric," her grandmother allusively answered, but faintly, and Pauline went on to the visitor: "And would one always enjoy oneself then?"

"Why not?" Mrs. Sammile said. "Everything lovely in you for a perpetual companion, so that you'd never be frightened or disappointed or ashamed any more. There are tales that can give you yourself completely and the world could never treat you so badly then that you wouldn't neglect it. One can get everything by listening or looking in the right way: there are all sorts of turns."

Phœbe reappeared by Mrs. Anstruther's chair. "Miss Fox and Mr. Stanhope, madam," she said, and retired with a message.

Pauline said, as she stood up, "It'd be too wonderful," and then, "Aren't you rather tired, grandmother? Wouldn't you rather go upstairs and let me see them indoors?"

"My dear," Mrs. Anstruther said, "as long as Peter Stanhope comes to see me, I shall receive him. At least, until Mrs. Sammile gives us the effect of Shakespeare without Shakespeare. Give me your arm."

She stood up, and leaning on the girl took a step or two forward, as Myrtle Fox, followed by Stanhope, came into the garden, and hurried across to her.

"Dear Mrs. Anstruther, how nice to see you again," Myrtle said. "It seems such a long time, but you know how rushed one is! But I felt I must come to-day. Do you know Mr. Stanhope? We met in the street and came along together."

Mrs. Anstruther allowed herself to be embraced and kissed without any further welcome than a smile; then she held out her hand.

"This is a great honour, Mr. Stanhope," she said. "I'm very glad to welcome you here."

He bowed over her hand. "It's very kind of you, Mrs. Anstruther."

"I've owed you a great deal for a long while now," she said, "and I can do no more than acknowledge it. But I'm grateful that I can do that. Do you know Mrs. Sammile?"

Stanhope bowed again; Myrtle let out a new gush of greeting and they all sat down.

"I really came", Stanhope said after a little interchange, "to ask Miss Anstruther if she had any preference in names."

"Me?" said Pauline. "What sort of names?"

"As the leader of the Chorus," Stanhope explained. "I promised Mrs. Parry I'd try and individualize so far—for the sake of the audience—as to give her a name. Myself, I don't think it'll much help the audience, but as I promised—I wondered about something French, as it's to be eighteenth century, La Lointaine or something like that. But Mrs. Parry was afraid that'd make it more difficult. No one would understand (she thought) why leaves—if they are leaves—should be *lointaine*. . . ."

He was interrupted by Myrtle, who, leaning eagerly forward, said: "O, Mr. Stanhope, that reminds me. I was thinking about it myself the other day, and I thought how beautiful and friendly it would be to give all the Chorus tree-names. It would look so attractive on the programmes, Elm, Ash, Oak —the three sweet trees—Hawthorn, Weeping Willow, Beech, Birch, Chestnut. D'you see? That would make it all quite clear. And then Pauline could be the Oak. I mean, the Oak would have to be the leader of the English trees, wouldn't he —or she?"

"Do let Mr. Stanhope tell us, Myrtle," Mrs. Anstruther said; and "You'd turn them into a cosy corner of trees, Myrtle," Pauline interjected.

"But that's what we want," Myrtle pursued her dream, "we want to realize that Nature can be consoling, like life. And Art —even Mr. Stanhope's play. I think all art is so consoling, don't you, Mrs. Sammile?"

Mrs. Anstruther had opened her mouth to interrupt Myrtle, but now she shut it again, and waited for her guest to reply, who said in a moment, with a slight touch of tartness, "I'm sure Mr. Stanhope won't agree. He'll tell you nightmares are significant."

62

"O, but we agreed that wasn't the right word," Myrtle exclaimed. "Or was it! Pauline, was it significant or symbolical that we agreed everything was?"

"I want to know my name," Pauline said, and Stanhope, smiling, answered, "I was thinking of something like Periel. Quite insignificant."

"It sounds rather odd," said Myrtle. "What about the others?"

"The others," Stanhope answered firmly, "will not be named."

"O!" Myrtle looked disappointed. "I thought we might have had a song or speech or something with all the names in it. It would sound beautiful. And Art ought to be beautiful, don't you think? Beautiful words in beautiful voices. I do think elocution is so important."

Pauline said, "Grandmother doesn't care for elocution."

"O, Mrs. Anstru——" Myrtle was beginning, when Mrs. Anstruther cut her short.

"What does one need to say poetry, Mr. Stanhope?" she asked.

Stanhope laughed. "What but the four virtues, clarity, speed, humility, courage? Don't you agree?"

The old lady looked at Mrs. Sammile. "Do *you*?" she asked.

Lily Sammile shrugged. "O, if you're turning poems into labours," she said. "But we don't all want to speak poetry, and enjoyment's a simple thing for the rest of us."

"We do all want to speak it," Stanhope protested. "Or else verse and plays and all art are more of dreams than they need be. They must always be a little so, perhaps."

Mrs. Sammile shrugged again. "You make such a business of enjoying yourself," she said with almost a sneer. "Now if I've a nightmare I change it as soon as I can." She looked at Pauline.

"I've never had nightmares since I Couéd them away," Myrtle Fox broke in. "I say every night: 'Sleep is good, and

63

sleep is here. Sleep is good.' And I never dream. I say the same thing every morning, only I say Life then instead of Sleep. 'Life is good and Life is here. Life is good.' "

Stanhope flashed a glance at Pauline. "Terribly good, perhaps," he suggested.

"Terribly good, certainly," Myrtle assented happily.

Mrs. Sammile stood up. "I must go," she said. "But I don't see why you don't enjoy yourselves."

"Because, sooner or later, there isn't anything to enjoy in oneself," Stanhope murmured, as she departed.

Pauline took her to the gate, and said good-bye.

"Do let's meet," Mrs. Sammile said. "I'm always about, and I think I could be useful. You've got to get back now, but sometime you needn't get back. . . ." She trotted off, and as she went the hard patter of her heels was the only sound that broke, to Pauline's ears, the heavy silence of the Hill.

The girl lingered a little before returning. A sense of what Miss Fox called "significance" hung in her mind; she felt, indeterminately, that something had happened, or, perhaps, was beginning to happen. The afternoon had been one of a hundred—the garden, a little talk, visitors, tea—yet all that usualness had been tinged with difference. She wondered if it were merely the play, and her concern with it, that had heightened her senses into what was, no doubt, illusion. Her hands lay on the top bar of the gate, and idly she moved her fingers, separating and closing them one by one for each recollected point. Her promise to her grandmother—death was not to interrupt verse; the memory of her ancestor—death swallowed up in victory—Struther's Salvation, Anstruther's salvation; elocution, rhetoric, poetry, Peter Stanhope, Lily Sammile, the slight jar of their half-philosophical dispute; her own silly phrase—"to make your own weather"; tales of the brain, tales to be told, tales that gave you yourself in quiet, tales or the speaking of verse, tales or rhetoric or poetry; "clarity, speed, courage, humility". Or did they only prevent desirable enjoyment, as Lily Sammile had hinted? One would have to be terribly good to achieve them. And terribly careful about the tales. She looked down the street, and for an instant felt that if she saw It coming—clarity, speed, courage, humility —she might wait. She belonged to the Chorus of a great experiment; a thing not herself.

> *The Magus Zoroaster, my dead child,*
> *Met his own image walking in the garden.*

If those four great virtues were needed, as Peter Stanhope had proposed, even to say the verse, might Shelley have possessed them before he discovered the verse? If she were wrong in hating them? if they had been offered her as a classification, a hastening, a strengthening? if she had to discover them as Shelley had done, and beyond them. . . .

She must go back. She pulled herself from the gate. Mrs. Sammile had just reached the corner. She looked back; she waved. The gesture beckoned. Pauline waved back, reluctantly. Before she told herself tales, it was needful to know what there was in verse. She must hear more.

She was not offered more. The visitors were on the point of departure, and Mrs. Anstruther was certainly tired. She roused herself to beg Stanhope to come again, if he would, but no more passed, except indeed that as Pauline herself said goodbye, Stanhope delayed a moment behind Miss Fox to add: "The substantive, of course, governs the adjective; not the other way round."

"The substantive?" Pauline asked blankly.

"Good. It contains terror, not terror good. I'm keeping you. Good-bye, Periel," and he was gone.

Later in the day, lying unsleeping but contented in her bed, Mrs. Anstruther also reviewed the afternoon. She was glad to have seen Peter Stanhope; she was not particularly glad to have seen Lily Sammile, but she freely acknowledged, in the words

E

of a too often despised poet, that since God suffered her to be, she too was God's minister, and laboured for some good by Margaret Anstruther not understood. She did not understand clearly what Mrs. Sammile conceived herself to be offering. It sounded so much like Myrtle Fox: "tell yourself tales".

She looked out of the window. There would be few more evenings during which she could watch the departure of day, and the promise of rarity gave a greater happiness to the experience. So did the knowledge of familiarity. Rarity was one form of delight and frequency another. A thing could even be beautiful because it did not happen, or rather the not-happening could be beautiful. So long always as joy was not rashly pinned to the happening; so long as you accepted what joys the universe offered and did not seek to compel the universe to offer you joys of your own definition. She would die soon; she expected, with hope and happiness, the discovery of the joy of death.

It was partly because Stanhope's later plays had in them something of this purification and simplicity that she loved them. She knew that, since they were poetry, they must mean more than her individual being knew, but at least they meant that. He discovered it in his style, in words and the manner of the words he used. Whether his personal life could move to the sound of his own lucid exaltation of verse she did not know. It was not her business; perhaps even it was not primarily his. His affair had been the powerful exploration of power after his own manner; all minds that recognized power saluted him. Power was in that strange chorus over which the experts of Battle Hill culture disputed, and it lay beyond them. There was little human approach in it, though it possessed human experience; like the *Dirge* in *Cymbeline* or the songs of Ariel in the *Tempest* it possessed only the pure perfection of fact, rising in rhythms of sound that seemed inhuman because they were free from desire or fear or distress. She herself did not yet dare to repeat the Chorus; it was beyond her courage. Those who had less knowledge or more courage might do so. She dared only to recollect it; to say it would need more courage than was required for death. When she was dead, she might be able to say Stanhope's poetry properly. Even if there were no other joy, that would be a reason for dying well.

Here, more than in most places, it should be easy. Here there had, through the centuries, been a compression and culmination of death as if the currents of mortality had been drawn hither from long distances to some whirlpool of invisible depth. The distances might be very long indeed; from all places of predestined sepulchre, scattered through the earth. In those places the movement of human life had closed—of human life or human death, of the death in life which was an element in life, and of those places the Hill on which she lived was one. An energy reposed in it, strong to affect all its people; an energy of separation and an energy of knowledge. If, as she believed, the spirit of a man at death saw truly what he was and had been, so that whether he desired it or not a lucid power of intelligence manifested all himself to him—then that energy of knowledge was especially urgent upon men and women here, though through all the world it must press upon the world. She felt, as if by a communication of a woe not hers, how the neighbourhood of the dead troubled the living; how the living were narrowed by the return of the dead. Therefore in savage regions the houses of sepulchre were forbidden, were taboo, for the wisdom of the barbarians set division between the dead and the living, and the living were preserved. The wisdom of other religions in civilized lands had set sacramental ceremonies about the dying, and dispatched the dead to their doom with prayers and rites which were not meant for the benefit of the dead alone. Rather, they secured the living against ghostly oppression; they made easy the way of the ghosts into their own world and hurried them upon their way. They were sped on with unction and requiem, with intercessions and masses; and the sword of exorcism waved at the portal of their exodus against the return of any whom those salutations of departure did not ease. But where superstition and religion failed, where cemeteries were no longer forbidden and no longer feared; where the convenient processes of cremation encouraged a pretence of swift passage, where easy sentimentality set up a pretence of friendship between the living and the dead—might not that new propinquity turn to a fearful friendship in the end? It was commonly accepted that the dead were anxious to help the living, but what if the dead were only anxious for the living to help them? or what if the infection of their experience communicated itself across the too shallow grave? Men were beginning to know, they were being compelled to know; at last the living world was shaken by the millions of spirits who endured that further permanent revelation. Hysteria of self-knowledge, monotony of self-analysis, introspection spreading like disease, what was all this but the infection communicated over the unpurified borders of death? The spirits of the living world were never meant to be so neighbourly with the spirits of that other. "Grant to them eternal rest, O Lord. And let light eternal shine upon them." Let them rest in their own places of light; far, far from us be their discipline and their endeavour. The phrases of the prayers of intercession throb with something other than charity for the departed; there is a fear for the living. Grant them, grant them rest; compel them to their rest. Enlighten them, perpetually enlighten them. And let us still enjoy our refuge from their intolerable knowledge.

As if in a last communion with the natural terrors of man, Margaret Anstruther endured a recurrent shock of fear. She recalled herself. To tolerate such knowledge with a joyous welcome was meant, as the holy Doctors had taught her, to be the best privilege of man, and so remained. The best maxim towards that knowledge was yet not the *Know thyself* of the Greek so much as the *Know Love* of the Christian, though both in the end were one. It was not possible for man to know himself and the world, except first after some mode of know-ledge, some art of discovery. The most perfect, since the most intimate and intelligent, art was pure love. The approach by love was the approach to fact; to love anything but fact was not love. Love was even more mathematical than poetry; it was the pure mathematics of the spirit. It was applied also and active; it was the means as it was the end. The end lived everlastingly in the means; the means eternally in the end.

The girl and the old woman who lay, both awake, in that house under the midnight sky, were at different stages of that way. To the young mind of Pauline, by some twist of grace in the operation of space and time, the Greek maxim had taken on a horrible actuality; the older vision saw, while yet living, almost into a world beyond the places of the dead. Pauline knew nothing yet of the value of those night vigils, nor of the fulfilment of the desire of truth. But Margaret had, through a long life, practised the distinction, not only between experience and experience, but in each experience itself between dream and fact. It is not enough to say that some experiences are drugs to the spirit; every experience, except the final, has a quality which has to be cast out by its other quality of perfection, expelled by healthy digestion into the sewers where the divine scavengers labour. By a natural law Margaret's spirit exercised freely its supernatural functions and with increasing clearness looked out on to the growing company of the Hill.

Lights in the houses opposite had long since been put out. The whole rise of ground, lying like a headland, or indeed itself like some huge grave in which so many others had been dug, was silent in the darkness, but for one sound; the sound of footsteps. Margaret knew it very .well; she had heard it on many nights. Sometimes in the day as well, when the peace was deepest within her and without, she could hear that faint monotonous patter of feet reverberating from its surface. Its distance was not merely in space, though it seemed that also, but in some other dimension. Who it was that so walked for ever over the Hill she did not know, though in her heart she did not believe it to be good. The harsh phrase would have been alien to her. She heard those feet not as sinister or dangerous, but only—patter, patter—as the haste of a search for or a flight from repose—perhaps both. Ingress and regress, desire and repulsion, contended there. The contention was the only equilibrium of that haunter of the Hill, and was pain. Patter, patter. It sounded at a distance, like the hurrying feet of the woman on her own garden path that afternoon. She had heard, in old tales of magic, of the guardian of the threshold. She wondered if the real secret of the terrible guardian were that he was simply lost on the threshold. His enmity to man and heaven was only his yearning to enter one without loss. It did not matter, nor was it her affair. Her way did not cross that other's; only it was true she never sank into those circles of other sensation and vision but what, far off, she heard —patter, patter—the noise of the endless passage.

There moved within her the infinite business of the Hill into which so much death had poured. First there came the creation of new images instead of those of every day. Her active mind still insisted on them; she allowed its due. The Hill presented itself before her with all its buildings and populace; she saw them, small and vivid, hurrying. She would even sometimes recognize one or other, for the briefest second. She had seen, in that re-creation by night of the Hill by day, Pauline going into a shop and Peter Stanhope talking in the street, and others. She remembered now, idly, that she had never seen the woman who had called on her that day, though she had seen Myrtle Fox running, running hard, down a long street. Distinct though the vision was it was but momentary.

It was the equivalent of her worldly affairs, and it lasted little longer; in a second it had gone.

It had enlarged rather. It reduplicated itself on each side, and its inhabitants faded from it as it did so, seeming themselves to pass into other hills. Presently there was no living form or building on that original Hill, and it was no longer possible to tell which had been the original, for a great range swept right across the sky, and all those heights were only the upper slopes of mountains, whose lower sides fell away beneath her vision. The earth itself seemed to lie in each of those mountains, and on each there was at first a populous region towards the summit, but the summit itself rose individual and solitary. Mountains or modes of consciousness, peaks or perceptions, they stood; on the slopes of each the world was carried; and the final height of each was a separate consummation of the whole. It was, as the apprehended movement upon each of them died away, in the time before the dawn that they rose there, nor had the sun risen, though they were not in darkness. Either a light emanated from themselves or some greater sun drew towards them from its own depth.

Then—it was not to say that they faded, but rather that she lost them, becoming herself one of them and ignorant of the rest. It was very silent; only small sounds came up to her as if someone was climbing below. The noises were so faint that in the air of earth they would have been lost. Had she been woman she would not have known them; now that she was not woman alone but mountain, the mountain knew that it was not from its own nature alone that the tiny disturbances came. There was movement within it certainly; rush of streams, fall of rocks, roar of winds through its chasms, but these things were not sound to it as was that alien human step. Through all another single note sounded once; a bell. Minutely she knew that the public clock of the Hill had struck one. It was a remote translation of a thing, for the dawn began.

## Vision of Death

It came from above, and as the light grew the mountain that was she became aware again of its fellows, spread out around no longer in a long range but in a great mass. They stretched away on all sides. At the increase of the sun there grew also an increase of fugitive sound; and she became aware of a few wandering shapes on the heights about her. Some climbed on; others, instead of welcoming the light as lost mountaineers should do, turned to escape it. They hurried into such caves or crevasses as they could find. Here and there, on a great open space, one lay fallen, twisting and dragging himself along. They seemed all, even those who climbed, grotesque obtrusions into that place of rock and ice and thin air and growing sun, a world different from theirs, hers and not hers. A divided consciousness lived in her, more intensely than ever before.

In the time of her novitiate it had seemed to her sometimes that, though her brains and emotions acted this way or that, yet all that activity went on along the sides of a slowly increasing mass of existence made from herself and all others with whom she had to do, and that strong and separate happiness—for she felt it as happiness, though she herself might be sad; her sadness did but move on it as the mountaineer on the side of a mountain—that happiness was the life which she was utterly to become. Now she knew that only the smallest fragility of her being clung somewhere to the great height that was she and others and all the world under her separate kind, as she herself was part of all the other peaks; and though the last fragility was still a little terrified of the dawn which was breaking everywhere, she knew that when the dawn reached the corner where she lay it would, after one last throb of piercing change under its power, light but the mountain side, and all her other mighty knowledge would after its own manner rejoice in it. She had not much strength in these days—that she which was Margaret Anstruther and lay in her bed on Battle Hill—but such as she had it was her business to use. She set herself to crawl out of that darkened corner towards the light. She turned from all the corner held —her home, her memories, Stanhope's plays, Pauline; with an effort she began her last journey. It might take hours, or days, or even years, but it was certain; as she moved, crawling slowly over the rock, she saw the light sweeping on to meet her. The moment of death was accepted and accomplished in her first outward movement; there remained only to die.

On her way and in her bed, she dozed a little, and in that light sleep—dream within dream or vision within vision—she seemed to be walking again in the streets of Battle Hill, as if, having renounced it, it was restored to her. It was still night there; the lamps were lit in the streets; the rustle of the many trees was substituted for the silence of the mountains. But the great mountains were there, and the light of them, and their inhabitants; though the inhabitants did not know the soil on which they lived. In a foretaste of the acute senses of death she walked among them, but they did not see her. Outside her own house she saw Pauline come out and look bitterly this way and the other, and start to walk down the road, and presently as if from the mountain side another Pauline had grown visible and came to meet the first, her head high and bright as the summit, her eyes bright with the supernatural dawn, her movements as free and yet disposed as the winds that swept the chasms. She came on, her feet which at first made no noise, beginning to sound on the pavement as she took on more and more of mortal appearance, and the first Pauline saw her and turned and fled, and the second pursued her, and far away, down the dark streets and round the dark mountain, they vanished from sight. And then again, and now she was not by her own house but in another street towards the top of the Hill, she saw a man walking hurriedly on, a man strange to her, but after him followed a crowd of others, young men and children, and all of them with his face. They pursued him, as the vision of Pauline had pursued the vision of Pauline, but this time with angry or plaintive cries, and he hurried on seeking something, for his restless eyes turned every way and sometimes he peered at the gutter and sometimes he looked up at the dark window, till presently he turned in at one of the gates, and about the gate his company seemed to linger and watch and whisper. Presently she saw him at a window, looking down; and there were at that window two forms who did not seem to see each other, but the second she knew, for he had been at her house once not so long ago, and it was Lawrence Wentworth. He too was looking down, and after a little he was coming out of the gate, and after him also came a figure, but this time a woman, a young woman, who pursued him in his turn, and for whom also he lay in wait.

But the other man too had now come out into the street, only it was no more the street of a town but a ruined stretch of scaffolding or bone or rock, all heights and edges and bare skeleton shapes. He was walking there on the mountain though he did not know it, any more than he noticed the light. He walked and looked up and round, and her eyes met his, and he made a sudden movement of wonder and, she thought, of joy. But as they looked, the dream, which was becoming more and more a dream, shifted again, and she heard quick and loud the patter-patter of those footsteps with which, as if they marked a region through or round which she·passed, such experiences always began and ended. She was on the Hill, and all the houses were about her, and they stood all on graves and bones, and swayed upon their foundations. A great stench went up from them, and a cry, and the feet came quicker, and down the street ran Lily Sammile, waving and calling, and checked and stood. She looked at a gate; Pauline was standing there. The two neared each other, the gate still between them, and began to talk. "No more hurt, no more pain, no more but dreams," a voice said. Margaret Anstruther put out a hand; it touched a projection in the rock on which she was lying in her journey towards corporeal death. She clung to it, and pulled herself forward towards Pauline. The nurse in the room heard her and turned. Mrs. Anstruther said: "I should like to see Pauline; will you ask her——" and at that she woke, and it was striking one.

## Chapter Five

# RETURN TO EDEN

**M**argaret Anstruther had seen, in her vision, a single
house, with two forms leaning from the same window. Time there had disappeared, and the dead
man had been contemporaneous with the living. As if simul-
taneity approached the Hill, the experiences of its inhabitants
had there become co-eval; propinquity no longer depended
upon sequence.

The chance that brought Lawrence Wentworth into such
close spiritual contact with the dead was the mere manner of
his ill luck. His was not worse than any other's, though the
hastening of time to its end made it more strange. It grew
in him, like all judgment, through his negligence. A thing of
which he had consistently refused to be aware, if action is the
test of awareness, drew close to him: that is, the nature of the
Republic. The outcast of the Republic had climbed a forlorn
ladder to his own death. His death entered into the Republic,
and into the lives of its other members. Wentworth had never
acknowledged the unity. He had never acknowledged the
victims of oppression nor the presence of victimization. It may
be that such victimization is inevitable, and that the Republic
after its kind must be as false to its own good as the lives of
most of its children are to theirs. But Wentworth had neither
admitted nor rejected this necessity, nor even questioned
and been hurt by it; he had merely ignored it. He had refused
the agony of the *res publica*, and of temporal justice. Another
justice sharpened the senses of his *res privata*. He was doubly
open to its approach—in his scholarship, where the ignoring
of others began to limit, colour, and falsify his work, and in

76

his awareness of supernatural neighbours, if any should be near. One was.

The dead man had stood in what was now Wentworth's bedroom, and listened in fear lest he should hear the footsteps of his kind. That past existed still in its own place, since all the past is in the web of life nothing else than a part, of which we are not sensationally conscious. It was drawing closer now to the present; it approached the senses of the present. But between them still there went—patter, patter—the hurrying footsteps which Margaret Anstruther had heard in the first circle of the Hill. The dead man had hardly heard them; his passion had carried him through that circle into death. But on the hither side were the footsteps, and the echo and memory of the footsteps, of this world. It was these for which Wentworth listened. He had come back into his own room after he had heard those steady and mocking footsteps of Hugh and Adela, and the voices and subdued laughter accompanying them. He had himself wandered up and down, and come to a rest at last at the finished window where, with no wall before him, the dead man had peered. He also peered. He listened, and his fancy created for him the unheard melody of the footsteps. His body renewed and absorbed the fatal knowledge of his desire. He listened, in the false faith of desire. It could not be that he would not hear, out of those double footsteps, one true pair separating themselves, coming up the street, approaching the gate; that he would not see a true form coming up the drive, approaching the door. It must happen; his body told him it must happen. He must have what he wanted, because . . . but still those feet did not come. The dead man stood by him, arm to arm, foot by foot, and listened, the rope in his hand, and that night neither of them heard anything at all.

The evening and the morning were the first day, of a few hours, or a few months, or both at once. Others followed. The business of the Hill progressed; the play went forward. Pauline

fled, and Margaret died, or lived in process of death. Hugh
went up and down to the City. Adela went about the Hill.
Wentworth, now possessed by his consciousness of her, and
demanding her presence and consent as its only fulfilment,
went about his own affairs. "Blessed is he whosoever shall not
be offended in Me"; the maxim applies to many stones of
stumbling, and especially to all those of which the nature is
the demand for a presence instead of the assent to an absence;
the imposition of the self upon complacency. Wentworth made
his spiritual voice hoarse in issuing orders to complacency,
and stubbed his toes more angrily every day against the unmovable stone.

Once or twice he met Adela—once at Mrs. Parry's, where
they had no chance to speak. They smiled at each other—an
odd smile; the faintest hint of greed, springing from the invisible nature of greed, was in it on both sides. Their greeds
smiled. Again he ran into her one evening at the post office—
with Hugh, and Hugh's smile charged theirs with hostility. It
ordered and subdued Adela's; it blocked and repulsed Wentworth's. It forced on him the fact that he was not only unsuccessful, but old; he contended against both youth and a
rival. He said: "How's the play going?"

"We're all learning our parts," Adela said. "There doesn't
seem to be time for *anything* but the play. Shall we ever get
another evening with you, Mr. Wentworth?"

He said: "I was sorry you could neither of you come."
That, he thought, would show that he hadn't been taken in.

"Yes," said Hugh; the word hung ambiguously. Wentworth,
angered by it, went on rashly: "Did you have a pleasant
time?"

He might have meant the question for either or both. Adela
said: "O well, you know; it was rather a rush. Choosing
colours and all that."

"But fortunately we ran into each other later," Hugh
added, "and we almost ran at each other—didn't we, Adela?—

so we fed in a hurry and dashed to a theatre. It might have been much worse."

Wentworth heard the steps in his brain. He saw Hugh take Adela's arm; he saw her look up at him; he saw an exchanged memory. The steps went on through him; double steps. He wanted to get away to give himself up to them: life and death, satisfaction of hate and satisfaction of lust, contending, and the single approach of the contention's result—patter, patter, steps on the Hill. He knew they were laughing at him. He made normal noises, and abnormally fled. He went home.

In his study he automatically turned over his papers, aware but incapable of the organic life of the mind they represented. He found himself staring at his drawings of costumes for the play, and had an impulse to tear them, to refuse to have anything to do with the grotesque mummery, himself to reject the picture of the rejection of himself. But he did not trust his own capacity to manage a more remote force than Adela— Mrs. Parry. Mrs. Parry meant nothing to him; she could never become to him the nervous irritation, the obsession, which both Aston Moffatt and Adela now were. His intelligence warned him that she was, nevertheless, one of the natural forces which, like time and space, he could not overcome. She wanted the designs, and she would have them. He could refuse, but not reject, Adela; he could reject, but he certainly could not refuse, Mrs. Parry. Irritated at his knowledge of his own false strength, he flung down the rescued designs. Under them were his first drafts; he tore them instead.

The evening wore into night. He could not bring himself to go to bed. He walked about the room; he worked a little and walked, and walked a little and worked. He thought of going to bed, but then he thought also of his dream, and the smooth strange rope. He had never so much revolted against it as now; he had never, waking, been so strongly aware of it as now. It might have been coiled in some corner of the room, were it not that he knew he was on it, in the dream. Physically and emotionally weary, he still walked, and a somnambulism of scratched images closed on him. His body twitched jerkily; the back of his eyes ached as if he stared interiorly from the rope into a backward abysm. He stood irritably still.

His eyes stared interiorly; exteriorly they glanced down and saw the morning paper, which, by an accident, he had not opened. His hands took it up, and turned the pages. In the middle he saw a headline: "Birthday Honours", and a smaller headline: "Knighthood for Historian". His heart deserted him: his puppet-eyes stared. They found the item by the name in black type for their convenience: "Aston Moffatt".

There was presented to him at once and clearly an opportunity for joy—casual, accidental joy, but joy. If he could not manage joy, at least he might have managed the intention of joy, or (if that also were too much) an effort towards the intention of joy. The infinity of grace could have been contented and invoked by a mere mental refusal of anything but such an effort. He knew his duty—he was no fool—he knew that the fantastic recognition would please and amuse the innocent soul of Sir Aston, not so much for himself as in some unselfish way for the honour of history. Such honours meant nothing, but they were part of the absurd dance of the world, and to be enjoyed as such. Wentworth knew he could share that pleasure. He could enjoy; at least he could refuse not to enjoy. He could refuse and reject damnation.

With a perfectly clear, if instantaneous, knowledge of what he did, he rejected joy instead. He instantaneously preferred anger, and at once it came; he invoked envy, and it obliged him. He crushed the paper in a rage, then he tore it open, and looked again and again—there it still was. He knew that his rival had not only succeeded, but succeeded at his own expense; what chance was there of another historical knighthood for years? Till that moment he had never thought of such a thing. The possibility had been created and withdrawn simultaneously, leaving the present fact to mock him. The other possibility—of joy in that present fact—receded as fast. He had determined, then and for ever, for ever, for ever, that he would hate the fact, and therefore facts.

He walked, unknowing, to the window, and stared out. He loomed behind the glass, a heavy bulk of monstrous greed. His hate so swelled that he felt it choking his throat, and by a swift act transferred it: he felt his rival choking and staggering, he hoped and willed it. He stared passionately into death, and saw before him a body twisting at the end of a rope. Sir Aston Moffatt . . . Sir Aston Moffatt. . . . He stared at the faint ghost of the dead man's death, in that half-haunted house, and did not see it. The dead man walked on his own Hill, but that Hill was not to be Wentworth's. Wentworth preferred another death; he was offered it.

As he stood there, imagining death, close to the world of the first death, refusing all joy of facts, and having for long refused all unselfish agony of facts, he heard at last the footsteps for which he had listened. It was the one thing which could abolish his anger; it did. He forgot, in his excitement, all about Aston Moffatt; he lost sight, exteriorly and interiorly, of the dangling figure. He stood breathless, listening. Patter— patter; they were coming up the road. Patter—patter; they stopped at the gate. He heard the faint clang. The footsteps, softer now, came in. He stared intently down the drive. A little way up it stood a woman's figure. The thing he had known must happen had happened. She had come.

He pushed the window up—careful, even so, not to seem to go fast, not to seem to want her. He leaned out and spoke softly. He said: "Is that you?" The answer startled him, for it was Adela's voice and yet something more than Adela's, fuller, richer, more satisfying. It said "I'm here." He could only just hear the words, but that was right, for it was after midnight, and she was beckoning with her hand. The single pair of feet drawn from the double, the hand waving to him. He motioned to her to come, but she did not stir, and at last,

driven by his necessity, he climbed through the window—
it was easy enough, even for him—and went down to meet
her. As he came nearer he was puzzled again, as he had been
by the voice. It was Adela, yet it was not. It was her height,
and had her movement. The likeness appeased him, yet he
did not understand the faint unlikeness. For a moment he
thought it was someone else, a woman of the Hill, someone
he had seen, whose name he did not remember. He was up
to her now, and he knew it could not be Adela, for even
Adela had never been so like Adela as this. That truth which
is the vision of romantic love, in which the beloved becomes
supremely her own adorable and eternal self, the glory and
splendour of her own existence, and her own existence no
longer felt or thought as hers but of and from another, that
was aped for him then. The thing could not astonish him, nor
could it be adored. It perplexed. He hesitated.

The woman said: "You've been so long."

He answered roughly: "Who are you? You're not Adela."

The voice said: "Adela!" and Wentworth understood that
Adela was not enough, that Adela must be something different.
even from Adela if she were to be satisfactory to him, something closer to his own mind and farther from hers. She had
been in relation with Hugh, and his Adela could never be in
relation with Hugh. He had never understood that simplicity
before. It was so clear now. He looked at the woman opposite
and felt a stirring of freedom in him.

He said: "You waved?" and she: "Or didn't you wave to
me?"

He said, under her eyes: "I didn't think you'd be any use
to me."

She laughed: the laugh was a little like Adela's, only better.
Fuller; more amused. Adela hardly ever laughed as if she were
really amused; she had always a small condescension. He said:
"How could I know?"

"You don't think about yourself enough," she said; the

words were tender and grateful to him, and he knew they were true. He had never thought enough about himself. He had wanted to be kind. He had wanted to be kind to Adela; it was Adela's obstinate folly which now outraged him. He had wanted to give himself to Adela out of kindness. He was greatly relieved by this woman's words, almost as much as if he had given himself. He went on giving. He said: "If I thought more of myself?"

"You wouldn't have much difficulty in finding it," she answered. "Let's walk."

He didn't understand the first phrase, but he turned and went by her side, silent while he heard the words. Much difficulty in finding what? in finding it? the it that could be found if he thought of himself more; that was what he had said or she had said, whichever had said that the thing was to be found, as if Adela had said it, Adela in her real self, by no means the self that went with Hugh; no, but the true, the true Adela who was apart and his; for that was the difficulty all the while, that she was truly his, and wouldn't be, but if he thought more of her truly being, and not of her being untruly away, on whatever way, for the way that went away was not the way she truly went, but if they did away with the way she went away, then Hugh could be untrue and she true, then he would know themselves, two, true and two, on the way he was going, and the peace in himself, and the scent of her in him, and the her, meant for him, in him; that was the she he knew, and he must think the more of himself. A faint mist grew round them as they walked, and he was under the broad boughs of trees, the trees of the Hill, going up the Hill, up to the Adela he kept in himself, where the cunning woman who walked by his side was taking him, and talking in taking. He had been slow, slow, very slow not to see that this was true, that to get away from Hugh's Adela was to find somewhere and somehow the true Adela, the Adela that was his, since what he wanted was always and everywhere his; he had always known that, yet that had been his hardship, for he must know it was so, and yet it hadn't seemed so. But here in the mists under the trees, with this woman, it was all clear. The mist made everything clear.

She said: "In here." He went in; a wooden door swung before and behind him.

It was quite dark. He stood. A hand slipped into his hand, and pressed it gently. It drew him forward, and a little to one side. He said aloud: "Where are we?" but there was no answer, only he thought he heard the sound of water running, gently, a lulling and a lapping. It was not worth while, against that sound, asking again where he was. The darkness was quiet; his heart ceased to burn, though he could hear its beating, in time with the lapping and lulling waters. He had never heard his heart beating so loudly; almost as if he were inside his own body, listening to it there. It would be louder then, he thought, unless his senses were lulled and dulled. Likely enough that if he were inside his own body his senses would be lulled, though how he got there or how he would get out. . . . If he wanted to get out. Why? Why fly from that shelter, the surest shelter of all, though he could not be quite there yet because of the hand that guided him, round and round in some twisting path. He knew that there were hundreds of yards, or was it millions, of tubes or pipes or paths or ropes or something, coiled, many coils, in his body; he would not want to catch his foot in them or be twisted up in them— that was why the hand was leading him. He pressed it, for acknowledgment; it replied. They were going downhill now, it seemed, he and his guide, though he thought he could smell Adela, or if not Adela, something like Adela, some growth like Adela, and the image of a growth spread in his brain to trees and their great heavy boughs; it was not a lapping but a rustling; he had come out of himself into a wood, unless he was himself and a wood at the same time. Could he be a wood? and yet walk in it? He looked at that question for a long time while he walked, and presently found he was not thinking of that but of something else; he was slipping his fingers along a wrist, and up an arm—only a little way, for he still wished to be led on the way, though everything was so quiet he could hardly think there was any need. He liked going on, away, away, away, from somewhere behind, or indeed outside, outside the wood, outside the body, outside the door. The door wouldn't open for anyone; it was his door, and though he hadn't fastened it, it wouldn't open, because it knew his wish, and his wish was to leave the two who had worried him outside the door. It was fun to think they were playing games on him when he wasn't there; running round under his windows, and he was quite away, and they would never know, even if he saw them again, where and how and why he had been. It was good for him to be here, and great fun; one day he would laugh, but laughter would be tiring here, under trees and leaves, leaves—leaves and eaves—eaves and eves; a word with two meanings, and again a word with two meanings, eves and Eves. Many Eves to many Adams; one Eve to one Adam; one Eve to each, one Eve to all. Eve. . . .

They stopped. In the faint green light, light of a forest, faint mist in a forest, a river-mist creeping among the trees, moon in the mist, he could just see the shape of the woman beside him. He might be back again in Eden, and she be Eve, the only man with all that belonged to the only man. Others, those whose names he need not then remember, because they were the waking animals of the world—others were inconsiderable to the grand life that walked now in this glade. They hardly belonged to it at all; they belonged outside, they were outside, outside the sealed garden, no less sealed for being so huge, through a secret gate of which he had entered, getting back to himself. He was inside and at peace. He said aloud: "I won't go back."

His companion answered: "You needn't go back *really*— or you can take it with you if you do. Wouldn't you like to?"

# Return to Eden

It took a while for this to reach him. He said, at last: "This? all this, d'you mean?" He was a little disturbed by the idea that he might have to go back among the shapes that ran about, harsh and menacing, outside the glade or the garden or the forest, outside the mist. They betrayed and attacked him. One had made fun of him and exposed him to her paramour. That was outside; inside, he knew the truth, and the truth was that she was quite subordinate to him. He breathed on her hand, and it was turned into stone, so that she couldn't carry it, but it sank to the ground, slowly, in that misty air, and she was held there, crying and sobbing, by the weight of her petrified hand. He would go away for a year or two, and perhaps when he came back he would decide to set her free by blowing on the stone hand. The whole air of this place was his breath; if he took a very deep breath, there would be no air left, outside himself. He could stand in a vacuum, and nothing outside himself could breathe at all, until he chose to breathe again; which perhaps he wouldn't do, so that he could infinitely prevent anything at all from existing merely by infinitely holding his breath. He held his breath for a century or so, and all the beasts and shapes of the wilderness, a tall young satyr and a plump young nymph among them, who were dancing to the music of their own chuckles, fell slowly down and died. The woman now beside him didn't die, but that was because she could live without air, of which he was glad, for he wanted her to go on living, and if she had needed air she would have died. He would have destroyed her without meaning to.

She was saying, eagerly: "Yes, yes, yes: better than Eve, dearer than Eve, closer than Eve. It's good for man to be alone. Come along, come along: farther in, farther in: down under, down under."

Down under what? down under where? down under the air that was or wasn't? but he was there under the air, on the point of breathing out everything that would be just right.

Why had he been so long content to have things wrong? it all came out of that silly name of Eve, which had prevented him realizing that he was what counted. Eve had never told him he had made her, and so he wouldn't make her again, she should be left all a twisted rag of skin in the vacuum, and he would have a world in which no one went to the City, because there was no City unless he—but no, he wouldn't have a City. Adela. . . .

He found he had been holding his breath; he released it. He found he was lying down, and that the woman was not there. He had exhaled, with a deep permission to Adela to exist. Now he was sleeping after that decision and act. He was awake in his sleep, and the moon was pouring itself over him. He wasn't on a rope now. The moon was pouring down, quite out of the sky; presently there wouldn't be any moon, only a hole in the sky: down, down! He felt hands moving over him, the moonlight changing to hands as it reached him, moon-hands, cool and thrilling. The hands were delighting in him; these were what he would take back to his own world, if he went. The moon would always be his, though all the moon-light had poured down now, and there was a hole, a dark hole, because the moon had emptied itself of its glory, and was not there any more; he was at first in the smallest degree troubled, for if odd things could disappear like this, could he be certain that his own Adela would live? yes, because he was a god, and sometime he would make another moon. He forgot it now; he was quite given up to the hands that caressed him. He sank into oblivion; he died to things other than himself; he woke to himself.

He lay quiet; beyond heart and lungs he had come, in the depth of the Hill, to the bottom of the body. He saw before him, in the disappearing moonlight, a place of cisterns and broad tanks, on the watery surface of which the moon still shone and from which a faint mist still arose. Between them, covering acres of ground, an enormous shape lay, something like a man's; it lay on its face, its shoulders and buttocks rose in mounds, and the head beyond; he could not see the legs lower than the thighs, for that was where he himself lay, and they could not be seen, for they were his own. He and the Adam sprang from one source; high over him he felt his heart beat and his lungs draw breath. His machinery operated, far away. He had decided that. He lay and waited for the complete creation that was his own.

The Adam slept; the mist rose from the ground. The son of Adam waited. He felt, coming over that vast form, that Hill of the dead and of the living, but to him only the mass of matter from which his perfect satisfaction was to approach, a road, a road up which a shape, no longer vast, was now coming; a shape he distrusted before he discerned it. It was coming slowly, over the mass of the Adam, a man, a poor ragged sick man. The dead man, walking in his own quiet world, knew nothing of the eyes to which his death-day walk was shown, nor of the anger with which he was seen. Wentworth saw him, and grew demented; was he to miss and be mocked again? what shape was this, and there? He sprang forward and up, to drive it away, to curse it lest it interpolated its horrid need between himself and his perfection. He would not have it: no canvassers, no hawkers, no tramps. He shouted angrily, making gestures; it offended him; it belonged to the City, and he would not have a City—no City, no circulars, no beggars. No; no; no. No people but his, no loves but his.

It still came on, slowly, ploddingly, wearily, but it came; on down the road that was the Adam in the bottom of Eden, determinedly plodding as on the evening when it had trudged towards its death, inexorably advancing as the glory of truth that broke out of the very air itself upon the agonized Florentine in the Paradise of Eden: "ben sem, ben sem, Beatrice"; the other, the thing seen, the thing known in every fibre to be not the self, woman or beggar, the thing in the streets of the City. No, no; no canvassers, no beggars, no lovers; and away, away from the City into the wood and the mist, by the path that runs between past and present, between present and present, that slides through each moment of all experience, twisting and twining, plunging from the City and earth and Eve and all otherness, into the green mist that rises among the trees; by the path up which she was coming, the she of his longing, the she that was he, and all he in the she—patter-patter, the she that went hurrying about the Hill and the world, of whom it was said that they whom she overtook were found drained and strangled in the morning, and a single hair tight about the neck, so faint, so sure, so deathly, the clinging and twisting path of the strangling hair. She whose origin is with man's, kindred to him as he to his beasts, alien from him as he from his beasts; to whom a name was given in a myth, Lilith for a name and Eden for a myth, and she a stirring more certain than name or myth, who in one of her shapes went hurrying about the refuge of that Hill of skulls, and pattered and chattered on the Hill, hurrying, hurrying, for fear of time growing together, and squeezing her out, out of the interstices, of time where she lived, locust in the rock; time growing together into one, and squeezing her out, squeezing her down, out of the pressure of the universal present, down into depth, down into the opposite of that end, down into the ever and ever of the void.

He was running down the path, the path that coiled round the edge of Eden, and the mist swooped to meet him. He had got right away from the road which was the shape of the Adam outstretched in the sleep precedent to the creation of fact, the separation of Eve, the making of things other than the self. He ran away into the comforting mist, partly because he liked it better, partly because there was nowhere else. He ran from sight; he found sensation. Arms met and embraced, a mouth kissed him, a sigh of content was loosed to him and from him. He was held, consoled, nourished, satisfied. Adela; he; sleep.

The door swung after him. He was standing on Battle Hill, not far from his house, but higher, towards the cemetery, towards the height. There, waiting for him, was a girl. She exactly resembled Adela. She came towards him softly, reached her hand to him, smiled at him, put up her mouth to him. It was night on the Hill. They turned together and went down it; after the single footsteps the double sounded again, his own and the magical creature's drawn from his own recesses: she in him, he in him. He was complacent; they went home.

*Chapter Six*

# THE DOCTRINE OF
# SUBSTITUTED LOVE

auline sat back in her chair, and her arms lay along its
arms. A rehearsal was taking place in the ground of the
Manor House, and she had ended her part in the first
act. She was free to watch the other performers, and to consider the play once more. By now they had all got more or
less accustomed to that speaking of verse aloud which our uneducated mouths and ears find so difficult, being less instructed
than the more universal Elizabethan must have been. Pauline
remembered again, with a queer sense of inferiority, that no
Elizabethan audience, gods or groundlings, can have felt any
shock of surprise or awkwardness at a play opening with a
high rhodomontade of sound. No modern audience would
put up with going to the first night of a new play to hear the
curtain sweep up on such an absurd and superb invocation as:

*Hung be the heavens with black; yield, day, to night;*
*Comets, importing change . . .*

and so on. On the other hand, they accepted plays beginning
with the most ordinary prose. Even rhodomontade demands
a peculiar capacity, and to lose its bravery perhaps hampers
some other bravery of the spirit; to lose even one felicity is to
be robbed of more than we have a right to spare. Certainly
Stanhope had spared them any over-whelming magniloquence;
his verse was subdued almost to conversation, though as she
listened and read and studied and spoke it, she became aware
that the rhythm of these conversations was a great deal more
speedy and vital than any she could ever remember taking

part in. All Mrs. Parry's efforts to introduce a stateli ess of manner into the Grand Ducal court, and a humorous but slow —O so slow—realism into the village, and an enigmatic meandering meditativeness into the Chorus could not sufficiently delay the celerity of the lines. Once or twice Stanhope, having been consulted, had hinted that he would rather have the meaning lost than too firmly explained, and that speed was an element, but after a great deal of enthusiastic agreement they had all gone on as before. She herself had been pleasantly ticked off by Mrs. Parry that very afternoon for hurrying, and as Stanhope hadn't interfered she had done her best to be adequately slow. It was some recompense to sit now and listen to Adela and Mrs. Parry arguing with, or at least explaining to, each other. Adela, true to her principles of massing and blocking, arranged whole groups of words in chunks, irrespective of line and meaning, but according to her own views of the emotional quality to be stressed. She had just unexpectedly broken one line with a terrific symbolical pause.

"I am," she said to her Woodcutter, and pausing as if she had invoked the Name itself and waited for its Day of Judgment to appear, added in one breath, "only the perception in a flash of love."

Pauline encouraged in herself a twinge of wonder whether there were anything Adela Hunt were less only; then she felt ashamed of having tried to modify the line into her own judgment, especially into a quite unnecessary kind of judgment. She knew little enough of Adela, and the result was that she lost the sound of the woodcutter's answer—"A peremptory phenomenon of love". She thought, a little gloomily, that malice could create a fair number of peremptory phenomena for itself, not perhaps of love, but easily enjoyable, like Myrtle Fox's trees. Malice was a much cosier thing than love. She was rather glad they were not doing the last act to-day; that act in which Periel—male or female, no matter!—spirit, only not spiritual—she—began and led the Chorus; and where everyone came in, on the most inadequate excuses, the Princess and her lover and the Grand Duke and the farmers and the banditti and the bear; and through the woods went a high medley of wandering beauty and rejoicing love and courtly intelligence and rural laughter and bloody clamour and growling animalism, in mounting complexities of verse, and over all, gathering, opposing, tossing over it, the naughting cry of the all-surrounding and overarching trees.

It troubled her now, as it had not done when she first read it, as it did not the others. She wondered whether it would have troubled her if, since the day of his first call, she had not sometimes heard her grandmother and Peter Stanhope talking in the garden. It was two or three weeks ago, since he had first called, and she could not remember that they had said anything memorable since except a few *dicta* about poetry—but everything they said was full and simple and unafraid. She herself had rather avoided him; she was not yet altogether prepared in so many words to accept the terror of good. It had occurred to her to imagine those two—the old woman and the poet—watching the last act, themselves its only audience, as if it were presented by the imagined persons themselves, and by no planned actors. But what would happen when the act came to an end she could not think, unless those two went up into the forest and away into the sounds that they had heard, into the medley of which the only unity was the life of the great poetry that made it, and was sufficient unity. Under the influence of one of those garden conversations she had looked up in her old school Shelley the lines that had haunted her, and seen the next line to them. It ran:

*That apparition, solo of men, he saw;*

and it referred, of course, to Zoroaster. But she couldn't, watching the play, refrain from applying it to Stanhope. This apparition, sole of men—so far as she had then discovered—

93

he had seen; and she went back to wonder again if in those three lines Shelley, instead of frightening her, was not nourishing her. Supposing—supposing—that in this last act Peter Stanhope had seen and imagined something more awful even than a vision of himself; supposing he had contemplated the nature of the world in which such visions could be, and that the entwined loveliness of his verse was a mirror of its being. She looked at the hale and hearty young man who was acting the bear, and she wondered whether perhaps her real bear, if she had courage to meet it, would be as friendly as he. If only the woodcutter's son had not learned the language of the leaves while they burned in the fire! There was no doubt about that speech: the very smell and noise of the fire was in it, and the conviction of the alien song that broke out within the red flames. So perhaps the phœnix cried while it burned.

Someone sat down in the next chair. She looked; it was Stanhope. Mrs. Parry and Adela concluded their discussion. Adela seemed to be modifying her chunks of words—sharpening ends and pushing them nearer till they almost met. Presumably Mrs. Parry was relying on later rehearsals to get them quite in touch, and even, if she were fortunate, to tie them together. The rehearsal began again. Stanhope said: "You were, of course, quite right."

She turned her head towards him, gravely. "You meant it like that then?" she asked.

"Certainly I meant it like that," he said, "more like that, anyhow. Do you suppose I want each line I made to march so many paces to the right, with a meditation between each? But even if I could interfere it'd only get more mixed than ever. Better keep it all of a piece."

"But you don't mind," she asked, "if I'm a little quicker than some of them?"

"I should love to hear it," he answered. "Only I think it's probably our business—yours and mine—to make our own feelings agreeable to the company, as it were. This isn't a

94

play; it's a pleasant entertainment. Let's all be pleasantly entertaining together. "

"But the poetry?" she said.

He looked at her, laughing. "And even that shall be Mrs. Parry's," he said. "For this kind of thing is not worth the fretfulness of dispute; let's save all that till we are among the doctors, who aren't fretful."

She said suddenly, "Would you read it to me again one day? is it too absurd to ask you?"

"Of course I'll read it," he said. "Why not? If you'd like it. And now in exchange tell me what's bothering you."

Taken aback, she stared at him, and stammered on her answer. "But—but——" she began.

He looked at the performers. "Miss Hunt is determined to turn me into the solid geometry of the emotions," he said. "But—but—tell me why you always look so about you and what you are looking for."

"Do I?" she asked hesitatingly. He turned a serious gaze on her and her own eyes turned away before it. He said, "There's nothing worth quite so much vigilance or anxiety. Watchfulness, but not anxiety, not fear. You let it in to yourself when you fear it so; and whatever it is, it's less than your life."

"You talk as if life were good," she said.

"It's either good or evil," he answered, "and you can't decide that by counting incidents on your fingers. The decision is of another kind. But don't let's be abstract. Will you tell me what it is bothers you?"

She said, "It sounds too silly."

Stanhope paused, and in the silence there came to them Mrs. Parry's voice carefully enunciating a grand ducal speech to Hugh Prescott. The measured syllables fell in globed detachment at their feet, and Stanhope waved a hand outwards.

"Well," he said, "if you think it sounds sillier than that. God is good; if I hadn't been here they might have done the

95

# The Doctrine of Substituted Love

*Tempest.* Consider—'Yea—all which—it inher-it—shall dis-solve. And—like this—insub-stantial pag-eant fa-ded.' O certainly God is good. So what about telling me?"

"I have a trick," she said steadily, "of meeting an exact likeness of myself in the street." And as if she hated herself for saying it, she turned sharply on him. "There!" she exclaimed. "Now you know. You know exactly. And what will you say?"

Her eyes burned at him; he received their fury undisturbed, saying, "You mean exactly that?" and she nodded. "Well," he went on mildly, "it's not unknown. Goethe met himself once—on the road to Weimar, I think. But he didn't make it a habit. How long has this been happening?"

"All my life," she answered. "At intervals—long intervals, I know. Months and years sometimes, only it's quicker now. O, it's insane—no one could believe it, and yet it's there."

"It's your absolute likeness?" he asked.

"It's me," she repeated. "It comes from a long way off, and it comes up towards me, and I'm terrified—terrified—one day it'll come on and meet me. It hasn't so far; it's turned away or disappeared. But it won't always; it'll come right up to me—and then I shall go mad or die."

"Why?" he asked quickly, and she answered at once, "Because I'm afraid. Dreadfully afraid."

"But," he said, "that I don't quite understand. You have friends; haven't you asked one of them to carry your fear?"

"Carry my fear!" she said, sitting rigid in her chair, so that her arms, which had lain so lightly, pressed now into the basket-work and her long firm hands gripped it as if they strangled her own heart. "How can anyone else carry my fear? Can anyone else see it and have to meet it?"

Still, in that public place, leaning back easily as if they talked of casual things, he said, "You're mixing up two things. Think a moment, and you'll see. The meeting it—that's one thing, and we can leave it till you're rid of the other. It's the

fear we're talking about. Has no one ever relieved you of that?
Haven't you ever asked them to?"

She said: "You haven't understood, of course. . . . I was a
fool. . . . Let's forget it. Isn't Mrs. Parry efficient?"

"Extremely," he answered. "And God redeem her. But
nicely. Will you tell me whether you've any notion of what
I'm talking about? And if not, will you let me do it for
you?"

She attended reluctantly, as if to attend were an unhappy
duty she owed him, as she had owed others to others and tried
to fulfil them. She said politely, "Do it for me?"

"It can be done, you know," he went on. "It's surprisingly
simple. And if there's no one else you care to ask, why not use
me? I'm here at your disposal, and we could so easily settle
it that way. Then you needn't fear it, at least, and then again
for the meeting—that might be a very different business if you
weren't distressed."

"But how can I not be afraid?" she asked. "It's hellish nonsense to talk like that. I suppose that's rude, but——"

"It's no more nonsense than your own story," he said.
"That isn't; very well, this isn't. We all know what fear and
trouble are. Very well—when you leave here you'll think of
yourself that I've taken this particular trouble over instead of
you. You'd do as much for me if I needed it, or for any one.
And I will give myself to it. I'll think of what comes to you,
and imagine it, and know it, and be afraid of it. And then,
you see, you won't."

She looked at him as if she were beginning to understand
that at any rate he thought he was talking about a reality, and
as she did so something of her feeling for him returned. It was,
after all, Peter Stanhope who was talking to her like this. Peter
Stanhope was a great poet. Were great poets liars? No. But
they might be mistaken. Yes; so might she. She said, very
doubtfully: "But I don't understand. It isn't *your*—you haven't
seen it. How can you——"

## The Doctrine of Substituted Love

He indicated the rehearsal before them. "Come," he said, "if you like *that*, will you tell me that I must see in order to know? That's not pride, and if it were it wouldn't matter. Listen—when you go from here, when you're alone, when you think you'll be afraid, let me put myself in your place, and be afraid instead of you." He sat up and leaned towards her. "It's so easy," he went on, "easy for both of us. It needs only the act. For what can be simpler than for you to think to yourself that since I am there to be troubled instead of you, therefore you needn't be troubled? And what can be easier than for me to carry a little while a burden that isn't mine?"

She said, still perplexed at a strange language: "But how can I cease to be troubled? will it leave off coming because I pretend it wants you? Is it your resemblance that hurries up the street?"

"It is not," he said, "and you shall not pretend at all. The thing itself you may one day meet—never mind that now, but you'll be free from all distress because that you can pass on to me. Haven't you heard it said that we ought to bear one another's burdens?"

"But that means——" she began, and stopped.

"I know," Stanhope said. "It means listening sympathetically, and thinking unselfishly, and being anxious about, and so on. Well, I don't say a word against all that; no doubt it helps. But I think when Christ or St. Paul, or whoever said *bear*, or whatever he Aramaically said instead of *bear*, he meant something much more like carrying a parcel instead of someone else. To bear a burden is precisely to carry it instead of. If you're still carrying yours, I'm not carrying it for you—however sympathetic I may be. And anyhow there's no need to introduce Christ, unless you wish. It's a fact of experience. If you give a weight to me, you can't be carrying it yourself; all I'm asking you to do is to notice that blazing truth. It doesn't sound very difficult."

"And if I could," she said. "If I could do—whatever it is

you mean, would I? Would I push my burden on to anybody else?"

"Not if you insist on making a universe for yourself," he answered. "If you want to disobey and refuse the laws that are common to us all, if you want to live in pride and division and anger, you can. But if you will be part of the best of us, and live and laugh and be ashamed with us, then you must be content to be helped. You must give your burden up to some-one else, and you must carry someone else's burden. I haven't made the universe and it isn't my fault. But I'm sure that this is a law of the universe, and not to give up your parcel is as much to rebel as not to carry another's. You'll find it quite easy if you let yourself do it."

"And what of my self-respect?" she said.

He laughed at her with a tender mockery. "O, if we are of that kind!" he exclaimed. "If you want to respect yourself, if to respect yourself you must go clean against the nature of things, if you must refuse the Omnipotence in order to respect yourself, though why you should want so extremely to respect yourself is more than I can guess, why, go on and respect. Must I apologize for suggesting anything else?"

He mocked her and was silent; for a while she stared back, still irresolute. He held her; presently he held her at com-mand. A long silence had gone by before he spoke again.

"When you are alone," he said, "remember that I am afraid instead of you, and that I have taken over every kind of worry. Think merely that; say to yourself—'he is being worried,' and go on. Remember it is mine. If you do not see it, well; if you do, you will not be afraid. And since you are not afraid. . . ."

She stood up. "I can't imagine not being afraid," she said.

"But you will not be," he answered, also rising, certainty in his voice, "because you will leave all that to me. Will you please me by remembering that absolutely?"

"I am to remember," she said, and almost broke into a

little trembling laugh, "that you are being worried and terrified instead of me?"

"That I have taken it all over," he said, "so there is nothing
left for you."

"And if I see it after all?" she asked.

"But not 'after all'," he said. "The fact remains—but see
how different a fact, if it can't be dreaded! As of course it can't
—by you. Go now, if you choose, and keep it in your mind till
—shall I see you to-morrow? Or ring me up to-night, say
about nine, and tell me you are being obedient to the whole
fixed nature of things."

"I'll ring up," she said. "But I . . . it sounds so silly."

"It is silly sooth," he answered, "and dallies with the
innocence of love. Real sooth, real innocence, real love. Go
with God." They shook hands, and slowly, looking back once,
just before she reached the lane, she went out of his sight.

Stanhope, turning his eyes from her parting figure, looked
at the rehearsal and then settled himself more comfortably in
his chair. A certain superficial attention, alert and effective
in its degree, lay at the disposal of anyone who might need it,
exactly as his body was prepared to draw in its long outstretched legs if anyone wanted to pass. Meanwhile he disposed the rest of his attention according to his promise. He
recollected Pauline; he visualized her going along a road,
any road; he visualized another Pauline coming to meet her.
And as he did so his mind contemplated not the first but the
second Pauline; he took trouble to apprehend the vision, he
summoned through all his sensations an approaching fear.
Deliberately he opened himself to that fear, laying aside for
awhile every thought of why he was doing it, forgetting every
principle and law, absorbing only the strangeness and the
terror of that separate spiritual identity. His more active mind
reflected it in an imagination of himself going into his house
and seeing himself, but he dismissed that, for he desired to
subdue himself not to his own natural sensations, but to hers

first, and then to let hers, if so it should happen, be drawn back into his own. But it was necessary first intensely to receive all her spirit's conflict. He sat on, imagining to himself the long walk with its sinister possibility, the ogreish world lying around, the air with its treachery to all sane appearance. His own eyes began to seek and strain and shrink, his own feet, quiet though actually they were, began to weaken with the necessity of advance upon the road down which the girl was passing. The body of his flesh received her alien terror, his mind carried the burden of her world. The burden was inevitably lighter for him than for her, for the rage of a personal resentment was lacking. He endured her sensitiveness, but not her sin; the substitution there, if indeed there is a substitution, is hidden in the central mystery of Christendom which Christendom itself has never understood, nor can.

Since he could not take, nor would have admitted, her hate and rejection, her passion was received into the lucidity of his own spirit. The experience itself, sharply as his body took it, was less sharp for him; not that he willed it so, but because his senses received their communication from within not from without, and there is in all holy imagination from goodwill a quality of greatness which purifies and stabilizes experience. His goodwill went to its utmost, and utmost goodwill can go very far. It went to all but actual vision, and it excluded his intellectual judgment of that vision. Had he been asked, at that moment, for his judgment, he would have answered that he believed sincerely that Pauline believed sincerely that she saw, but whether the sight was actual or not he could not tell. He would have admitted that it might be but a fantastic obsession of her brain. That made no difference to his action. If a man seems to himself to endure the horrors of shipwreck, though he walks on dry land and breathes clear air, the business of his friend is more likely to be to accept those horrors as he feels them, carrying the burden, than to explain that the burden cannot, as a matter of fact, exist. Given all reasonable talk as well, wherever there is intelligence enough for exchange and substitution to exist, there is place enough for action. Only when the desire of an obsession has carried its subject beyond the interchanges of love can the power of substituted love itself cease. It would have been small use for any adept, however much greater than Peter Stanhope, to have offered his service to Wentworth, where he sat in his own room with the secret creature of substantial illusion at his feet caressing his hand; for from that haunting, even while it was but an unmaterialized anguish within his blood, Wentworth had had no desire, more than the desire of maddened pride, to be exquisitely free.

So devoted to the action of his spirit, Stanhope sat on among the sounds of laughter and gaiety and half-serious wrangles that rose around him. It was not a long while that he was left to sit alone; perhaps Pauline had not more than partly advanced on her return when someone came across to interrupt and consult him. He gave a full attention, for that other concern is not measured by time but by will. To give freedom to both, he would return to his task when opportunity next offered; afterwards, when they had all gone away, and he was alone. But that was rather for the sake of his own integrity of spirit than that more was needed. The act of substitution was fully made; and if it had been necessarily delayed for years (could that have been), but not by his fault, still its result would have preceded it. In the place of the Omnipotence there is neither before nor after; there is only act.

Pauline went out through the open door of the house, for the Manor was now almost a public building of happiness, and began to make her way towards her home. Just as she left, one of the other girls, who was only then arriving for her part, had delayed her with a question, a minute matter about a borrowed pattern for a dress, and possible alterations. Pauline also had given her attention, and now, walking down the road, went on thinking of it—and whether Mary Frobisher would really be well advised to move the left seam an eighth of an inch back, considering Mary Frobisher's figure. It was another thing for her, and the hang of the frock had been as satisfactory as could be hoped. But Mary—she stopped to smell the pinks in a garden she was passing. Pinks were not very showy flowers, but they had a fragrance. It was perhaps a pity they had so few in their own garden; she had once or twice thought of asking her grandmother to order the gardener to get some more, since the gardener certainly wouldn't otherwise do it. But Mrs. Anstruther was always so content with immediate existence that it seemed a shame to bother her about proximate existence. Pauline wondered if she, when she was ninety-seven, would be as little disturbed by the proximate existence of death as her grandmother seemed to be. Or would she be sorry to be compelled to abandon the pleasant wonder of this world, which, when all allowances were made, was a lovely place, and had——

She nearly came to a full stop; then, with slackened steps, she went on, blinking at the sunlight. She realized she had been walking along quite gaily. It was very curious. She looked down the road. Nothing was in sight—except a postman. She wondered whether anything would come into sight. But why was she so careless about it? Her mind leapt back to Stanhope's promise, and she knew that, whatever the explanation might be, she had been less bothered for the past ten minutes than ever before in any solitude of twenty years. But supposing the thing came? Well, then it came, but till it came why suppose it? If Peter Stanhope was taking trouble, as he was, because he said he would, there was no conceivable reason for her to get into trouble. She had promised to leave it to him; very well, she would. Let him—with all high blessing and gratitude—get on with it. She had promised, she had only to keep her promise.

So she put it to herself, but within herself she knew that, except just to ratify her promise, even that act of her mind was superfluous. It was an act purely of extra delight, an occasion of obedience. She wouldn't worry; no, because she couldn't worry. That was the mere truth—she couldn't worry. She was, then and there, whatever happened later, entirely free. She was, then and there incapable of distress. The world was beautiful about her, and she walked in it, enjoying. He had been quite right; he had simply picked up her parcel. God knew how he had done it, but he had. A thing had, everywhere and all at once, happened. A violent convulsion of the laws of the universe took place in her mind; if this was one of the laws, the universe might be better or worse, but it was certainly quite different from anything she had ever supposed it to be. It was a place whose very fundamentals she had suddenly discovered to be changed. She hadn't any clear idea of what Stanhope was doing, and that didn't matter, except that she ought, as soon as possible, to find out and try to understand. That was merely her duty, and might—the thought crossed her mind and was gone—be her very great happiness. Meanwhile, she would go on walking. And if she came to her self, well she came to her self. No doubt Peter Stanhope would be doing something about it. A kitten on a wall caught her eye; it put its head down; she stretched her arm and stood on tiptoe to stroke it, and so doing for a while she forgot Stanhope and the universe and Pauline.

The rehearsal had long been over, and the Manor left again to its owner. Stanhope had returned to his own proper activity of work, when, exactly as the clock in his study chimed nine, the telephone bell rang.

He took up the receiver.

"Peter Stanhope speaking," he said.

"Pauline," said a voice. "You told me to ring you up."

"I was waiting for you," he answered. "Well?"

"Well . . . there was a kitten and pinks and a pattern for a frock and a postman who said the rain was holding off," said the voice, and paused.

"Cautious man," said Stanhope, and waited.

"Well . . . that was all," the voice explained.

"Really all?" Stanhope asked.

"Really all," the voice answered. "I just went home. It *is* real, I suppose?"

"Entirely," said Stanhope. "Aren't you sure of it?"

"Yes, O, yes," said the voice. "It . . . I . . . I wanted to thank you. I don't know what you did——"

"But I've told you," he murmured, and was cut short.

"——but I did want to thank you. Only—what happens now? I mean—do I——" It stopped.

"I should think you did," said Stanhope, gravely. "Don't you? It seems a perfectly good idea."

"Ah, but do you mean that?" she protested. "It looks so like taking advantage."

"You'll be as involved morally as you are verbally, if you talk like that," he said. "Taking advantage! O my dear girl! Don't be so silly! You've got your own job to do."

"What's that?" she asked.

"Being ready to meet it," he answered. "It'll be quite simple, no doubt, and even delightful. But if I were you I'd keep my faculties quiet for that. If meeting is a pleasure, as we so often tell people, you may as well enjoy the pleasure."

"I hadn't really thought of it being that," said the voice.

"But now?" he asked.

"Yes . . . I . . . I suppose it might," she said.

"Do you see any reason whatever why it shouldn't? Since we're agreed you won't have any opportunity to be afraid," he added.

"It's funny," she said, after another pause, "but do you know I feel as if I'd never really looked at it till now. At least, perhaps the first time, when I was quite small, but I was always shut up when I talked about it, and then sometimes I saw it when . . . when I didn't like it. . . ."

"I don't quite follow," Stanhope said. "When you didn't like it?"

He couldn't see the blush that held Pauline as she sat by the telephone table, but he heard the voice become smaller and softer as she said, "When I wasn't being very good. There wasn't much money in the house, and once there was a shilling my mother lost, and then there were sweets. It was just after I'd bought the sweets that I saw it coming once. It was horrid to see it just then, but it was beastly of me, I know."

"Well, that's as may be," Stanhope said. "The limits of theft are a high casuistical problem. Read Pascal and the Jesuits—especially the Jesuits, who were more ordinary and more sensible. The triumph of the bourgeois."

"But I knew it was wrong," Pauline exclaimed.

"Still your knowledge may have been wrong," Stanhope demurred. "However, don't let's argue that. I see what you mean. Self-respect and all that. Well, it won't do you any harm to feel it knows you. Much the best thing, in fact."

"Y—yes," Pauline said. "Yes—I do think so really. And I'm not to worry?"

"You are most emphatically to remember that I'll do the worrying," Stanhope said. "Ring me up at any time—day or night; only if no one answers at night remember that, as Miss Fox so rightly told us, sleep is good, and sleep will undoubtedly be here. But sleep isn't separation in the Omnipotence. Go in peace, and wish me the same, for friendship's sake."

"O how can I?" she said, startled. "How can I wish peace to you? You are peace."

"M'm," Stanhope said. "But the more if you will have it so. Try."

"Good night then," she answered slowly. "Good night. Thank you. Go . . . in peace."

Her voice had faltered so that she could hardly speak the words, and when she rose from her seat she was on fire from head to foot. Guilt or shame, servile fear or holy fear, adoration

106

or desperation of obedience, it burned through her to a point of physical pain. The blood rode in her face and she panted a little in the heat. She could not have answered, had anyone spoken to her; her tongue seemed to have said its last words on earth. Never, never, her heart sang, let her speak again, never let the silence that followed her daring, her presumptuous invocation, be broken. It had been compelled, she had been commanded; a god had been with her—not Peter Stanhope, but whatever answered him from her depth.

She looked at her watch; it was not yet time for her evening visit to her grandmother. She looked round; a book lay on the table. It was the volume of Foxe with the account of her ancestor's martyrdom; Mrs. Anstruther had been reading it again. She walked to it, and with one hand, the knuckles of the other pressed against her slowly cooling cheek, turned the pages to find the place. Something from it was vaguely coming to her mind. "They set him to the stake and put the fire to the wood, and as the fire got hold of him he gave a great cry and said, *I have seen the salvation of my God.* . . . The Lord had done great things for him there in the midst of the fire." The Lord, she thought, made a habit of doing things in the midst of a fire; he had just brought her to say "Go in peace" in another. She glowed again to think of it. But it was the first phrase she had looked for; "I have seen the salvation". It had never occurred to her, any time she had read or remembered the martyrdom, that Struther was anything but a demented fanatic; a faint distaste that she should come of his blood had touched her. It now occurred to her that Struther might have been talking flat realism. She put the book down, and looked out of the window. It was—all of a sudden—remarkably easy to look out of the window. She might even walk down to the gate and look at the street. The parcel was completely in some one else's care, and all she had to do was to leave it. She hoped it was not troublesome to Peter Stanhope, but it wouldn't be. He and whatever he meant by the Omnipotence would manage it quite well between them. Perhaps, later on, she could give the Omnipotence a hand with some other burden; everyone carrying everyone else's, like the Scilly Islanders taking in each other's washing. Well, and at that, if it were tiresome and horrible to wash your own clothes and easy and happy to wash someone else's, the Scilly Islanders might be intelligent enough. "Change here for Scilly," she said aloud as she came to the gate.

"My dear!" said a voice beside her.

Pauline jumped. It was a fairly high wall, and she had been preoccupied; still, she ought to have seen the woman who was standing outside, alone against the wall on her left. For a moment something jarred, but she recovered. She said, "Oh, good evening, Mrs. Sammile. I didn't see you."

The other peered at her. "How's your grandmother?" she asked.

"Rather weaker, I'm afraid," Pauline said. "It's kind of you to ask."

"And how are you?" Lily Sammile went on. "I've been——" but Pauline unintentionally cut through the sentence.

"Very well indeed," she murmured, with a deep breath of pleasure. "Isn't it a lovely night?"

The other woman strained a little forward, as if, even in the June evening, she could not see her clearly. She said, "I haven't seen you about lately: you haven't wanted to see me. I thought perhaps you might."

Pauline looked back smiling. How, in this quietness of spirit, could she have thought she wanted anything changed? But the old lady had wanted to help, and though now she did not need the help, the goodwill remained. She said, leaning over the gate: "Oh, I'm much better now."

"That's good," the other woman said. "But take care of yourself. Think of yourself; be careful of yourself. I could make you perfectly safe and perfectly happy at the same time. You really haven't any idea of how happy you could be."

# The Doctrine of Substituted Love

Her voice was infinitely softer than Pauline could remember it. In the full light of day, the other woman had seemed to her slightly hard, her voice a light third hammer to her feet. She pattered everywhere, upstairs, downstairs, in my lady's chamber, in any chamber; but now her figure was dim and her feet still, and her voice soft. As soft as the dust the evening wind was blowing down the street. Dust of the dead, dust of the Struther who had died in flame. Had he been happy? happy? happy? Pauline was not sure whether she or her companion had spoken the word again, but it hung in the air, floating through it above, and the dust was stirred below, and a little dizziness took her and passed. Lazily she swung the gate.

She said, as if to draw down the floating mist: "Happy? I . . . I happy?"

The other murmured: "Happy, rich. Insatiate, yet satisfied. How delicious everything would be! I could tell you tales that would shut everything but yourself out. Wouldn't you like to be happy? If there's anything that worries you, I can shut it away from you. Think what you might be missing."

Pauline said: "I don't understand."

The other went on: "My dear, it's so simple. If you will come with me, I can fill you, fill your body with any sense you choose. I can make you feel whatever you'd choose to be. I can give you certainty of joy for every moment of life. Secretly, secretly; no other soul—no other living soul."

Pauline tingled as she listened. Shut up within herself—shut up till that very day with fear and duty for only companions—with silence and forbearance as only possibilities—she felt a vague thrill of promised delight. Against it her release that day began already to seem provisional and weak. She had found calm, certainly; only ten minutes earlier that calm had seemed to her more than she could ever have hoped. She loved it still; she owned to it this interval of indulgent communion with something other than calm. The communion threatened the calm with a more entrancing sensation of bliss;

she felt almost that she had too rashly abandoned her tribula-
tion for a substitute that was but a cold gift, when warm
splendour had been waiting to enrapture her. In the very
strength of her new-found security she leaned from it, as from
the house itself; as within a tower of peace, with deliberate
purpose she swung the gate more wide. Inconceivably she all
but regretted the fear that would have been an excuse, even
a just reason, for accepting a promise of more excitement of
satisfaction than peace and freedom could give or could excuse.
Peace had given her new judgment, and judgment began to
lament her peace. If she opened the gate, if the far vision of her
returning vision gave her speed and strength to leap from it
to this more thrilling refuge! And while her heart beat more
quickly and her mind laboured at once to know and not to
know its desires, a voice slid into her ear, teasing her, speeding
her blood, provoking her purpose. It spoke of sights and sounds,
touches and thrills, and of entire oblivion of harm; nothing
was to be that she did not will, and everything that she willed,
to the utmost fullness of her heart, should be. She would be
enough for herself. She could dream for ever, and her dreams
should for ever be made real. "Come soon," it said, "come now.
I'll wait for you here. In a few minutes you'll be free, and then
you'll come; you shall be back soon. Give me your hand and
I'll give you a foretaste now." A hand came into hers, a pulse
against her wrist beat with significance of breathless abandonment to delirious joy. She delayed in a tremulous and pleasurable longing.

"But how?" she murmured, "how can all this happen? how
do I know what I want? I've never thought . . . I don't know
anyone . . . and to be alone. . . ."

"Give me your hand," the other said, "then come and
dream, till you discover, so soon, the ripeness of your dreams."
She paused, and added, "You'll never have to do anything
for others any more."

It was the last touch, and false, false because of the habit

of her past and because of Stanhope's promise. The fountain
of beauty had sprung upward in a last thrust; it broke against
the arched roof of his world, and the shock stung her into
coldness. Never have to do anything—and she had been
promising herself that she would carry someone's parcel as hers
had been carried, that she would be what he said she could.
Like it or not, it had been an oath; rash or wise it stood.

"An oath, an oath, I have an oath in heaven." She had
been reading more verse of late, since she had had to speak
Stanhope's, and the holy words engulfed her in the sound
which was so much more than she. "An oath, an oath. . . .
Shall I lay perjury upon my soul?" The wind, rising as if to a
storm, screamed "perjury" through the sky that held the
Hill and all; false, false! she perjured in that last false gleam.
She was come; "false, fleeting, perjured Clarence! Seize on
him, Furies". . . . The word, Antæan, sprang hundred-voiced
around her, and held her by every gripping voice. Perjury, on
her soul and in her blood, if now she slipped to buy sweets with
money that was not hers; never, till it was hers in all love
and princely good, by gift and gift and gift beyond excelling
gift, in no secrecy of greed but all glory of public exchange,
law of the universe and herself a child of the universe. Never
till he—not Pascal nor the Jesuits nor the old chattering pat-
tering woman but he; not moonlight or mist or clouding dust
but he; not any power in earth or heaven but he or the peace
she had been made bold to bid him—till they bade her take
with all her heart what nothing could then forbid. An oath, an
oath, an oath in heaven, and heaven known in the bright
oath itself, where two loves struck together, and the serene
light of substitution shone, beyond her understanding but not
beyond her deed. She flung the gate shut, and snatched her
hands away, and as it clanged she was standing upright, her
body a guard flung out on the frontier of her soul. The other
woman was at the gate—of garden or world or soul—leaning
to but not over it, speaking hurriedly, wildly, and the voice

rising on the wind and torn and flung on the wind: "Everything, anything; anything, everything; kindness to me . . . help to me . . . nothing to do for others, nothing to do with others . . . everything, everything. . . ."

The door behind her was opened; the maid's voice said doubtfully: "Miss Pauline?"

Pauline, rigid at her post, said, turning her head a little: "You wanted me?"

Phœbe murmured: "Your grandmother's asking for you, Miss Pauline, if you could come."

Pauline said, "I'm coming." She looked over the gate; she added in a voice hard with an unreasoning hostility: "Good night." She ran in.

## Chapter Seven

# JUNCTION OF TRAVELLERS

The dead man walked in his dead town. It was still, quiet and deserted; he too was quiet in it. He had now, for long, no need to worry. Nagging voice and niggling hunger were gone. It was heaven enough; he sought nothing else. Dead or alive, or neither dead nor alive, he was free from the sick fear which the Republic had imposed on him. The stigmata of his oppression burned and ached no more. His tired feet had lightness; his worn form energy. He did not know or care if he were in the body or out of the body. For the first time he needed nothing, and nothing distressed him. He walked, sat, stretched himself out. He did not sleep, for he did not need sleep. Sometimes he wondered a little that he was never hungry or thirsty. It was an odd place he was in, but he did not grow tired of it any more than of walking through it. So much the better if he were not hungry or thirsty or tired. As for luxuries, he could not have missed them, for he had never had them, nor, then and there, was it permitted him to feel any want.

The faint light persisted. Time had no measurement except by the slow growth of his interior quiet, and to him none. All the capacities of satisfaction in one ordinary life, which have their fulfilment in many ways, in him there were concentrated on that quiet. Monotony could not exist where all duration was a slow encouragement of rest. Presently he even found himself looking up into the sky for the moon. The moon in his mind was, since his death, connected with the world he had known, with his single room and his wife, his enemies and tyrants. He felt, now safe, from it; he seriously expected its appearance, knowing that he was free. If the big pale ball had floated up, a balloon in which everything harmful was borne away, busy, but not with him, he would have been mildly pleased. He knew that that balloon was for ever cut off from him. Moon, balloon, it could not drop anyone among these shells of houses. If it did, whoever it dropped would be caught in the shells. He had been a good-tempered little victim, but there were one or two in the past whom he could placidly have borne to see scrabbling and thrusting at the scaffolding and cage. He did not exactly resent, in that quiet, anything they had done—a foreman, a mate, a brother, a wife, but perhaps, as the unmeasured time did pass, he felt a little more strongly that he would enjoy his freedom more if he saw them defeated. In the past they had taken everything from him. It would not be unpleasant now to see them raging with a wish to get at him, and, in that air, defeated.

He sat opposite his ladder, after a long, long while, and let the fancy grow. It was then that he first noticed a change. The light was growing stronger. It was, again, a long while between the first faintest hint of it and any notice he took, and again between his first faint wonder and his belief, and again between belief and certainty. At the end of all those long periods, there was not much perceptible difference in the sky. Centuries passed before that difference grew more marked, but that too came. He had sat watching it, dimly, peacefully. He rose then, not quickly but more quickly than he had been used to move. He stirred with a hardly discernible unease.

It seemed as if the light were spreading steadily down, from somewhere away in the height. He did not positively see that any patch of sky was whiter than the rest, but he was looking for such a patch. The increase must have a centre of expansion. It must come from somewhere. No moon, no sun, no cause of illumination. Only sometimes a kind of wave of movement passed down the sky, and then it was lighter. He did not like it.

If he had asked himself why, he could not have easily answered. It did not disturb his quiet. He was as lonely and peaceful as before. No sound was in his City, foot or voice. But vaguely the light distracted him from his dim pleasure of imagining, imagining disappointment. His imagination could hardly, by ordinary standards, be said to be good or bad. It was a pleasure in others' anger, and bad; but the anger was that of tyrannical malice, and the imagined disappointment of it was good. Some such austere knowledge the Divine John saw in heaven, where disappointed hell is spread and smokes before the Lamb. But the Lamb and the angels do not imagine hell to satisfy their lust, nor do he nor the angels determine it, but only those in hell; if it is, it is a fact, and, therefore, a fact of joy. In that peace which had been heaven to the vagrant, he had begun to indulge a fancy of his own; he went beyond the fact to colour the fact.

Light grew. He began to walk. He had done so, often enough, through that great period of re-creation, for pure pleasure of change. Now he had, for the first time, a purpose unacknowledged. He wished to escape the light. It was desirable that he should still be left alone. He did not trust the light to let him alone. It was desirable that he should be free to make pictures for himself and to tell himself tales. He did not trust the light to let him do it. He moved gently; there was no need, here, to run. The need that was not concealed from him, his first inclination to run. He had run often enough for others' pleasure, but this was the first time he had been tempted to run for his own. The light still gently spread. As gently he went away from it, down the hill. His choice was in this direction; it was brightest, by a little, at the top.

As, through a still unmeasured period, he went drifting, changes came on the hill. He did not at first notice them. Long as he had wandered, he had not marked detail of building there. But, unnoticed, details had altered. It was now a town half-built, not ruined. When he had climbed that skeleton shape of a house, or of himself, he had done so in the midst of a devastation. As he went away from it towards the bottom the devastation became incomplete erection. Houses were unfinished, roads unmade, yet they were houses and roads. Roofs were on, scaffolding gone. The change was irregular, more as if some plants had outgrown others than as if order had been established by man. He went soundlessly down the slope of the thickening vegetation, and as on the bare height the light was fullest, so here instead of light, shadows grew thicker. Between them the pallid light of his experience grew stronger by contrast. He would not look at the new light; there was increased for him by opposition the presence of the old.

He had gone some way, and some time, unnoticing, inclined to linger upon his tales and dreams, when he was startled into knowledge. He had turned his back upon light and had not remarked erection. He saw suddenly, at a distance in front of him, a flash. He stopped and stared. It was no longer a flash but a gleam. He was looking at, far off, the reflection of light upon glass—of what he would, in lost days, have called the sun upon a window.

A thrust of fear took him; he could not, for a moment, go on. He stood blinking; after a while, he turned his head. There was behind him a long space of shadows and pale light, but beyond that, away beyond the house where he had died, there was a broad stretch of high ground, bare and rocky, rising higher than he had ever thought, and all bright with, he supposed, the sun. A rich, golden splendour, beyond all, at the height of all, played flashing upon some other glittering surface; it was not glass there, but ice. He stared back as he had stared forward. He could not dare return to *that*, also he was unwilling to go on down towards the gleaming window below. That meant the world; he could not, after so much peace, return to the world. Why could he not sit and imagine a moon and thwarted creatures dropped from the moon into a world that mocked them? It was not much to ask.

It was too much; he could not have it. False as the Republic had been to him, making his life dreadful, he had not deserved, or he could not have, an infinity of recompense. He could not have this in utter exchange for that. Exchange had been given; temporal justice, for what it is worth, done. Now incidents were no more counted, on this side or the other. He must take the whole—with every swiftness of the Mercy, but the whole he must have.

He saw that the exhibition of light was moving towards him. It had reached the house where he had died. He noticed, even in his alarm, that the buildings now ended there. In his earlier wanderings he had gone among the ruins both above and below it, but now the bare rock rose above—or ice, as he had first thought. It went up, in blocks and irregularities of surface, until, some distance beyond, it opened on one broad sweep, smooth and glittering, rounding towards the top of the Hill; upon it, by some trick of sight, the sunlight seemed active. It was not changed, but it ran. It hastened in sudden charges of intensity, now across, now down. The unchanging rock beneath the unchanging sun responded to that counter-marching, evoked into apparent reordination. It was perhaps this which terrified him, for there the earth was earth still and yet alive. In the strict sense of the words it was living stone.

He stood for some minutes staring, and entranced. But at some sudden charge downwards from the height towards the house, and him beyond it, he broke. He gave a little cry, and ran. He ran down towards the bottom of the Hill, among the houses, towards that house where the glass was. As he ran he saw, for the first time since he had entered that world, other forms, inhabitants of a state for which there were no doubt many names, scientific, psychological, theological. He did not know the names; he knew the fact.

The return of time upon itself, which is in the nature of death, had caught him. Margaret Anstruther had, in a vision within a dream, decided upon death, not merely in her own world but in that other. Her most interior heart had decided, and the choice was so profound that her past experiences and her present capacities could only obey. She had no work of union with herself to achieve; that was done. But this man had died from and in the body only. Because he had had it all but forced on him, he had had opportunity to recover. His recovery had brought to him a chance of love. Because he had never chosen love, he did not choose it then. Because he had never had an opportunity to choose love, nor effectively heard the intolerable gospel proclaimed, he was to be offered it again, and now as salvation. But first the faint hints of damnation were permitted to appear.

He was running down a street. It was a street that closed in on him. He did not notice, in his haste, that it was a street much like those in which most of his life had been spent. He saw, in front of him, at a great distance, two living forms, a man and a girl; at which he ran with increased speed. Since he had begun to go down the Hill he had lost his content in being alone; he smelt solitude as if it were the odour of bare rock, and he hated it. He heard, more vividly with every step, no sound. He could not hear those forms walking, but he saw them; it was enough; he ran. He was catching them up, running very fast through his old life to do it. When he was within a hundred yards the girl looked over her shoulder. He checked in midpace, his foot heavily thudding down, and he almost falling. He saw, with sharp clarity, the face of the girl who had been his wife. Her mouth was opening and shutting on words, though the words were silent. It had always been opening and shutting. At once, without looking round, the figure arm in arm with hers released itself, stopped, and as if moving by the direction of that busily talking mouth, took a step or two backwards. Then it paused, and with a weary care began slowly to turn itself round. The dead man saw the movement. It became terribly important that he should escape before the youth he had been caught him and dragged him in, to make a third with them, and to listen again to that hated and loathed voice—always perhaps; the prisoner of those two arms, the result and victim of his early desire. He ran hastily back again up the street.

Presently he glanced behind him, and could not see them. He trotted a little farther, looked round again, saw the street still empty—the street that was recovering the appearance of a street upon the Hill—and dropped to a walk. Only he could not go on right to the end, though he had come thence, for he could see across it a beam of faint but growing sun, as the ocean beams at the end of a road. He did not think of the image, for he had not seen the sea, since his childhood; and that time would not be remembered until he reached it. An instinct, none the less, warned him; so he did not make his way to where, ready for him, in that twisting maze of streets and times, a gutter child played on his only seaside holiday, and cried because a bigger boy had bullied him. Sea or sun—sun to him—it was the light he wished to avoid. He hesitated, and took a side turning, where under the eaves some darkness was left.

The image was growing more complex and more crowded, for, as if the descending light, the spreading harshness of rock and ice, crowded them and the streets grew shorter, more involved, themselves more populous with figures. Once it was a sneering foreman, who drove his face-hidden shape towards him; once—how he got there he did not know—it was someone's back on a ladder carrying a rope, going up no doubt, but perhaps coming down to throw the rope round him before he slipped away. Once he turned from a figure leaning against a lamp-post, quite still, with a stealthy suspense, as if it might dodge round the lamp-post, pretending that the post hid what it could not hide, and making to play a game that was not a kind game. And each time he slipped away or turned away, it was more like running away, and continually he would see, here and there in the distance, the beam of light on icy rock and sniff the bitter smell of the place of no return.

So presently he was running very quickly, with a sense that they were now after him. They had begun to be bolder, they were leaning out of windows, stumbling out of streets, lurching, shambling, toiling after him. He had read somewhere of a man being trampled to death, and he thought of that now; only he could not envisage death, any more than Pauline the end of luxurious dream. He could only think of trampling. He ran faster then, for he did not see how he would ever be able to get up, those apparitions of his terror would be too many and too strong. For the first time in that world he began to feel exhausted; and now the streets were slipping by, and the feet were coming up, and in a central daze in that dance of time and truth all round him, he felt himself stopping. He dimly consented; he stood still.

As he did so, there came about him also a cessation. The street was still; the feet silent. He drew a breath. He saw in front of him a house, and at a window, a window with glass where no light gleamed, he saw a face, the face of an old woman, whom never in all his life had he seen before. He saw her as a ghost in the shadow, within the glass, but the glass was only a kind of faint veil—of ceremony or of habit, though he did not think of it so. He felt it did not matter, for he and the other were looking directly at each other. He wanted to speak; he could not find words to utter or control. He broke into a cry, a little wail, such as many legends have recorded and many jokes mocked. He said: "Ah! ah!" and did not think it could be heard.

The old face looked at him, and he was trembling violently, shaking to see the apparition of this world's living, as they shake to see the phantasms of the dead. He knew he was not afraid, as they are often afraid; this was almost the first face he had seen, in the body or out of the body, of which he was not afraid. Fear, which separates man from man, and drives some to be hostile, and some tyrannical, and some even to be friendly, and so with spirits of that state of deathly time, there abandoned him. Fear, which never but in love deserts mortal man, deserted him there. Only he could not do or say any more. He stared, hungrily, hopefully. He waited, selfishly certain she would go, sweetly sure she would stay. She said, as he waited: "My dear, how tired you look!"

To Margaret herself the images were becoming confused. She did not, for a good part of the time, know of any, being engaged merely, beyond her own consciousness, in passing through that experience which in her dream had meant crawling over the stretch of open rock. Some hint of memory of it recurred to her at moments. She had on this evening known nothing but a faint sense of slow dragging in her limbs, an uneasiness in her body as if it lay rough, a labouring in her breath as if she toiled. Then she had felt herself lying on rock, holding a spike of rock, and instinctively knew she had to do something, and clasped the spike with energy—it had to do with Pauline; and a bell—the great bell of the dead, or the bell of the living on the Hill, or her own little bell, or all at once—had rung; and as it did so, she saw a strange face looking at her from a crevice of darkness below. Then she knew it; it was the face of the strange man in her dream. She was aware that Pauline was coming over the rock through a door of great stones like Stonehenge, but Pauline was behind, and across in front of a gleam of mountain light that pierced her room was the shadow of the weary and frightened face. She said with a fresh spring of pure love, as if to Pauline or Phœbe or anyone: "My dear, how tired you look!"

He tried to answer, to thank her, to tell her more, to learn salvation from her. His life, in and out of the body, had forgotten the time when a woman's voice had last sounded with friendship in his ears. He wanted to explain. This face was neither light nor darkness but more tolerable and deeper than either, as he felt it, for it had lived towards him in love. He made efforts to speak, and seemed to himself to do no more than cry out again, wordlessly and wailingly. The sound he made communicated his fear, and she answered him from her withdrawn experience of death, as from his less withdrawn spirit of poetry Stanhope had answered Pauline—nothing could be worth such distress. Or nothing, at least, but one thing—the coming out of it into tender joy. She said: "But wait: wait for it."

Pauline had come in from the garden, and as she ran through the hall she was furiously angry with herself. She did not very well know what the woman in the street had offered, beyond indefinable sweet and thrilling excitements. But she felt, her foot on the first stair, that she had regretted, that she had grudged and been aggrieved with, the new change in her life. She had almost, if by God's mercy not quite, wished that Peter Stanhope had not interfered. No range of invective—and she had a pretty, if secret, range—sufficed her for herself. She struck her hand against the wall as she ran, and wished that it was her head, or that someone—Stanhope for preference, but it didn't much matter; anyone would do—would pick her up and throw her violently over the banisters to the floor below, knocking the breath out of her body, and leaving her bruised and gasping, looking like the fool she was. She put all herself into despising herself, and her scorn rode triumphant through her: a good thing under direction, but dangerous to the lonely soul. So ambiguously repentant, she came into her grandmother's room, and saw suddenly that the justice of the universe had taken her earlier word and abandoned her.

It was not so, but at the window there was a face; and she had, in the first shock, supposed it was hers. The obsession of her visitation returned, through the double gate of her repining and her rage. It was coming, it was come, it was here. Her wild spirit sickened in her; and as she felt its power dissolve, she sprang to the other power the knowledge of which, at least, her anger had preserved. Ashamed of betrayal, unashamed of repentence and dependence, she sprang. She knew with all her soul's consent that Peter Stanhope had taken over her fear; was, now, one with it; and it was not, for he was in power over it. Among the leaves of his eternal forest he set it, and turned it also to everlasting verse. Evading or not evading, repining or not repining, raging or not raging, she was Periel; she was the least of the things he had created new; *ecce, omnia nova facio.* She was a line of his verse, and beyond that—for the thought of him took that high romantic self-annihilation and annihilated it in turn—she was herself in all freedom and courage. She was herself, for the meeting with herself. She stepped forward—lightly, almost with laughter. It was not yet she.

As she gazed, she heard her grandmother speak. The room, for those three spirits, had become a place on the unseen mountain: they inhabited a steep. The rock was in them, and they in it. In Margaret Anstruther it lived; it began to put out its energy of intellectual love. At least to the dead man it was felt as love, as love that loved him, as he longingly and unknowingly desired. This holy and happy thing was all that could be meant by God: it was love and power. Tender to the least of its creatures, it submitted itself to his need, but it is itself always that it submits, and as he received it from those eyes and the sound of that voice he knew that another thing awaited him—his wife, or the light, or some renewal of his earlier death. Universal, it demanded universality. The peace communicated there was of a different kind from the earlier revival of rest. And the woman said: "It's done already; you've only got to look for it."

As Pauline had moved forward, the face at the window disappeared from her sight. She drew breath; it had been an accident of light; there had been no face. She turned to look at her grandmother, and saw her lying very still, her eyes on the window as if she could still see something there. Quiet as she lay, she was in action. Her look, her voice, showed it: her voice, for she spoke, but very low, and Pauline could not hear the words. She caught the sound; lightly she threw herself on her knees by the bed—and half fulfilled her earlier passionate desire for subordination. For the first time in her young distracted life her energy leapt to a natural freedom of love. She ran swiftly down the way her master had laid open; she said, in words almost identical with his: "Let me do something, let me carry it. Darling, do let me help." Margaret gave her hand a small gentle pressure, but kept her eyes beyond her still.

The silence in that place became positive with their energies, and its own. The three spirits were locked together, in the capacity of Margaret's living stone. The room about them, as if the stillness expressed its nature in another mode, grew sharply and suddenly cold. Pauline's mind took it as the occasional sharp alteration of a summer evening; she moved to go and turn on the electric fire, for fear her grandmother should feel the chill, and that natural act, in her new good will, was no less than any high offer of goodness and grace. But Margaret knew the other natural atmosphere of the icy mountain, where earthly air was thin in the life of solitude and peak. It was the sharp promise of fruition—her prerogative was to enter that transforming chill. The dead man also felt it, and tried to speak, to be grateful, to adore, to say he would wait for it and for the light. He only moaned a little, a moan not quite of pain, but of intention and the first faint wellings of recognized obedience and love. All his past efforts of good temper and kindness were in it; they had seemed to be lost; and they lived.

But that moan was not only his. As if the sound released something greater than itself, another moan answered it. The silence groaned. They heard it. The supernatural mountain on which they stood shook and there went through Battle Hill itself the slightest vibration from that other quaking, so that all over it china tinkled, and papers moved, and an occasional ill-balanced ornament fell. Pauline stood still and straight. Margaret shut her eyes and sank more deeply into her pillow.

The dead man felt it and was drawn back away from that window into his own world of being, where also something suffered and was free. The groan was at once dereliction of power and creation of power. In it, far off, beyond vision in the depths of all the worlds, a god, unamenable to death, awhile endured and died.

## Chapter Eight

# DRESS REHEARSAL

Among the many individualized forms, dead or living, upon the Hill, there was one neither dead nor living. It was the creature which had lingered outside the illusion of Eden for the man who had consented to its company. It had neither intellect nor imagination; it could not criticize or create, for the life of its substance was only the magical apparition of its father's desires. It is said in the old tales that the devil longs to become incarnate that he may challenge the Divine Word in his own chosen house of flesh and that he therefore once desired and overshadowed a maid. But even at the moment of conception a mystical baptism fell on the child, and the devil was cast out of his progeny at the moment of entrance. He who was born of that purified intercourse with angelic sacrilege was Merlin, who, wisest of magicians, prophesied and prefigured the Grail-quest, and built a chapel to serve the Table till Logres came to an end, and the Merciful Child Galahad discovered the union in a Mass of the Holy Ghost which was sung by Messias among a great company of angels. Since that frustrating transubstantiation the devil has never come near to dominion over a mortal woman. His incubi and succubi which tempt and torment the piety of anchorites, are phantasms, evoked from and clouded and thickened with the dust of the earth or the sweat of the body or the shed seed of man or the water of ocean, so as to bewilder and deceive longing eyes and eager hands.

The shape of Lawrence Wentworth's desire had emerged from the power of his body. He had assented to that making, and again, outside the garden of satisfied dreams, he had

assented to the company of the shape which could not be
except by his will and was imperceptibly to possess his will.
Image without incarnation, it was the delight of his incarnation for it was without any of the things that troubled him
in the incarnation of the beloved. He could exercise upon it all
arts but one; he could not ever discover by it or practise towards it the freedom of love. A man cannot love himself; he
can only idolize it, and over the idol delightfully tyrannize—
without purpose. The great gift which this simple idolatry of
self gives is lack of further purpose; it is, the saints tell us, a
somewhat similar thing that exists in those wholly possessed
by their End; it is, human experience shows, the most exquisite
delight in the interchanges of romantic love. But in all loves
but one there are counterpointing times of purposes; in this
only there are none.

They had gone down the hill together, the man and that
creature of illusion which had grown like the flowers of
Eastern magic between the covering and uncovering of a seed.
The feminine offspring of his masculinity clung to him, pressing
her shoulder against him, turning eyes of adoration on him,
stroking his fingers with her own. The seeming trance prolonged
itself in her in proportion as it passed from his own senses;
he could plunge again into its content whenever the creature
looked at or spoke to him. Their betrothal had been celebrated
thus before they began to walk down the hill, and in that
betrothal a fraction of his intelligence had slept never to wake.
During the slow walk his child dallied with his senses and
had an exquisite perception of his needs. Adela walked by
him and cajoled him—in the prettiest way—to love her. He
was approached, appeased, flattered, entreated. There flowed
into him from the creature by his side the sensation of his
absolute power to satisfy her. It was what he had vehemently
and in secret desired—to have his own way under the pretext
of giving her hers. This was the seed which grew in his spirit
and from which in turn his spirit grew—the core of the fruit

and also the fruit of the core. The vagrant of matter murmured to him; it surrounded him with devotion, as very well it could, seeing what the only reality of its devotion was. He did not need to say much, nor himself to initiate approach. It took all that activity upon itself; and the sweet reproaches which its mouth offered him for having misunderstood and neglected and hurt it were balm to his mind. He had hurt her—then he had not been hurt or she did not know it. He was wanted—then he need not trouble to want or to know he wanted. He was entreated by physical endearments—in languorous joy he consented to gratify the awful ambiguity of his desire.

At his own gate they had paused. There, for a little, he almost recovered himself; his habitual caution leapt into action. He thought for himself: "Suppose anyone saw us?" and looked anxiously up at the windows. They were dark; his servants were asleep in their own rooms at the back of the house. He glanced up and down the road; no one was about. But his caution, having struck one note, passed to another; he looked down at the creature who stood opposite him. It was Adela in every point, every member and article: its hair, its round ears, its full face, its plump hands, its square nails, its pink palms, its gestures, its glances. Only that appealing softness was new, and by that same appealing softness he knew clearly for an instant that it was not Adela who had returned by his side.

He stared at it and a shudder seized him; he took a half-step away, and the first chance of escape was offered. He wondered, desperately, perhaps in a little hope, if it would say good-night and go away. His hand was on the latch of the gate, yet he hesitated to do anything so certain as to go sharply through. He looked up and down the street; perhaps someone would come. He had never before wanted to see Hugh Prescott; now he did. If Hugh would come and slip his arm through Adela's and take her away! But Hugh could not save him unless he wanted the thing that was Hugh's, and not this

other thing. The thought of Hugh had done all it could when
it reminded him of the difference between the real and the
unreal Adela. He must face jealousy, deprival, loss, if he
would be saved. He fled from that offer, and with a sudden
snarl clutched his companion by the arm. It leaned closer
to him, and otherwise circumstance lay still. It yearned to him
as if it feared to be disappointed, which indeed at the bottom
of his heart he infinitely did. It put one hand upon his heart.
It said, in a breathless whisper: "You won't send me away?"
Adela and his refusal to know Adela in relation to Hugh rose
in him; sensuality and jealousy twined. He swung open the
gate. It said: "Be kind to me, be whatever you want, but
don't send me away." He had never been able to dream of a
voice so full of passion and passion for him. The hand that
smoothed his heart was the hand that had lain in Hugh's,
yet it was not; he crushed it in his own, relieved from agony
and released to a pretended vengeance. His mind became
giddy. He caught the whole form tighter, lest indeed Hugh
should come striding out of the night, tall as a house, and
stretch out a huge animal hand, and pull her from his arm.
He moved to the threshold; as if it swooned against him it
drooped there with all its weight upon his heart and side.
He muttered thickly: "Come on, come on," but it seemed
past movement. Its voice still murmured incoherent passion,
but its limbs were without strength to take the step. He said:
"Must I carry you?" and the head fell back, and the voice
in a trance of abandonment answered: "Carry me, carry me."
He gathered it to his arms and lifted it; it lay there, no more
than an easy weight.

As he moved, his mind spoke, or more than his mind. The
whole air of the Hill said in his ear, with a crisp intelligence:
"You fool, that's not Adela; you couldn't carry Adela. What
do you think you'll get out of anything that isn't Adela?"
He recognized well enough that the real Adela might have
given him considerable trouble to lift, but his whole damnation

was that he would not choose the trouble to lift the real Adela. This thing was light in his arms, though solid to his heart, and his brain was dazed by its whispers. He came over the threshold, and when they had entered the garden it found its feet again, and went along with him to the complacency of his dream.

Since that night it had come to him often, as on that night it had been all he could desire. It had been an ape of love's vitality, and a parody also of its morality. It possessed a semblance of initiative, and it had appeased, as is all lovers' duty, the fantasies of his heart; it had fawned on him and provoked him. He had no need of the devices against fertility which, wisely or unwisely, the terrible dilemmas of men drive them to use, for he consummated a marriage whose infertility was assured. This, which it made clear to him for his satisfaction, a little troubled him, for it reminded him, until he managed to forget, of its true nature. He was outraging his intelligence with this invited deceit, and he did not wish to know it. But it passed, for he was given good measure after his kind. There was no lack of invention and pleasure, for the other forming of sterile growth from sterile root was far off, lying in the necessity of the stir of distant leaves on the side of the mountain where he had no thought to come.

The days went by, and still he was consoled. In the mornings it had gone; in the early summer dawns it wakened him to whisper farewells, and his heavy drugged sleep only understood that here also it was fulfilling his need. He had not at first very clearly understood why or where it was going, but he did not then care, for it promised him, leaning naked over him, that it would always return. Whether it were then Adela or a being like Adela he was too full of slumber to care; it was going; he need not trouble; for whenever he needed her, it would return. If it were Adela, she ought to get away; if it were not Adela, it ought still to go away, because there would be the morning and the world. . . . So much his drowsiness let through to him; and it went, showing him itself, in a faithful copy of his half-realized wishes, to the end. For contenting him with its caution, it gathered up the articles of its apparent dress, and presently all clothed it stole across the room, and by the door it turned, and with one gesture promised him itself again. In the dawn, at once by that gesture clothed and unclothed, it had shone before him, a pale light burning against the morning, the last flickering fire of the corpse-candles of the insubstantial; then it had passed, and left him to sleep. So when later they brought him his early tea, he was alone; but that day while he drank, he found the thought of the Adela of past days a little disagreeable—no longer troublesome or joyous but merely disagreeable. He would have to meet her, no doubt, one day; meanwhile he was entirely at peace, and he did not want to think of anything at all. He lay and drank, and was still.

As the days went by, he found that his child kept her promise. He could not conceive a way of coming that, sooner or later, she did not take, nor a manner of love that, sooner or later, she did not fulfil. Since it was more and more Adela, he was instinctively careful never to conceive a meeting which conflicted with the possibilities of the actual Adela; he asked of his nightly bedfellow nothing but secret advents or accidental encounters. But these gradually he multiplied; and always it answered. By chance, in the street, at first by late night, but afterwards earlier. For once this Adela said to him, in a casual phrase, to which only his own veiled knowledge gave a double meaning: "They won't remember if they see me." So he dared to walk with it sometimes for variation, but then they went always through the lower darker streets of the Hill, and at first they met no one whom he knew, and presently no one at all. But Adela Hunt wondered sometimes why she never seemed to run against Lawrence Wentworth by chance in the streets of Battle Hill.

Yet, in the order of the single universe known to myriads of minds, the time and place that belongs to each of those

myriads has relation to others; and though the measurement
of their experiences may differ, there is something common
to them all in the end. Sometimes where time varies place is
stable; or where places intermingle time is secure, and sometimes the equilibrium of both, which is maintained in so many
living minds, swings into the place of the dead. Sometimes the
dead know it, and sometimes the living; a single clock ticks
or a single door opens in two worlds at once. The chamber of
that dark fundamental incest had had the dead man for its
earliest inhabitant, though his ways and Wentworth's had
been far apart—as far as incest from murder, or as self-
worship from self-loathing, and either in essence false to all
that is. But the self-worship of the one was the potential
source of cruelty, as the self-loathing of the other was the
actual effect of cruelty; between them lay all the irresolute
vacillations of mankind, nourishing the one and producing
the other. All who had lived, or did or could live, upon Battle
Hill, leaned to one or the other, save only those whom holy
love had freed by its revelation of something ever alien from
and conjoined with the self.

In Wentworth's old dream he had climbed down a rope
securely and not unpleasantly, much as the world of our
culture sways on the rope from the end of which the outcasts
of civilization swing in a strangled life. Since the phantom of
Adela had come to him the dream had disappeared. He slept
deeply. If he woke she would be there by his side, petting or
crooning to him; until one night he thought how pleasant it
would be to wake and look on her asleep, and the next time
he woke, there indeed she was, disposed to his wish. But he
found it troubled him; as he looked at her in the silence he
began to wonder, and to think of the other Adela sleeping in
her own house. For a little he tried to find pleasure in considering how in effect he possessed her without her knowledge
or will, but the effort was too much for his already enfeebled
mind. He found himself disliking the life of the actual Adela;

he could be so happy with the substance by him if only the other were dead. But to know that she did not know . . . and that perhaps one day Hugh. . . . He had forgotten Hugh in these last weeks, and in a hasty retreat to oblivion he woke the creature from its apparent slumber, and in its yearnings and embraces lost actuality again and lost himself. He whispered to her then that she must never sleep when he woke, so drawing another veil between himself and the truth.

It was some nights afterwards that the dream returned. For the first time it troubled him. He was climbing in the darkness down that shining rope of silver, even more peacefully than ever he had climbed before. He was descending, he now vaguely imagined, towards a companion who waited for him far below, where the rope was fastened to the side of a cave in an unseen wall. The companion had waited, was waiting, would wait; it would never grow tired either of him or of waiting for him; that was why it was there, with its soft bare arms, and its sweet eyes closed in the dream of his approach. As he descended, in that warm expectation, a terrible sound broke on him. The abyss groaned. From above and below, from all sides, the rending grief of a hardly tolerable suffering caught him; he clung horribly to his rope, and the rope shook in the sound. The void became vocal with agony; the hollow above and the hollow below came together in that groan of the very air, and it echoed from unseen walls, and re-echoed, and slowly died. Only once it came. It was succeeded by the ancient silence. He listened breathlessly, but it did not recur. It had turned the dream into a nightmare for him; he shook on his rope, and struggled in his body, and so he awoke, and there by his side, waking also, was the companion he sought. He clutched it and hid himself against it; he hid his ears between its breasts and its hands, lest the night should groan again. In his haste to hide himself, as if like others he bade the mountains fall on him and the hills cover him, and in the darkness of the room, he did not see the inhuman countenance. It had grown haggard and old; its fullness fell away; its eyes were blurred. The meaning which he had given it had departed; an imbecile face stared blankly over him. The movements its body made were sufficient to cover his distress, but they had been jerky and inorganic, as if an automaton repeated its mechanical motions, and as if the mechanism were running down. For less than the time it took him to find refuge with her the creature that lay there was millions of years older than the dying woman by whom Pauline watched, while the pain of a god passed outwards from the mountain depths, as from those where Prometheus hung, or downwards from the cross that stood upon a hill that also was of skulls. It united itself with all spiritual anguish that received and took part with it; it fell away from the closed ears in the beds of Gomorrah. The dead man looked at Margaret, Pauline thought of Stanhope and was at peace as it ceased. The renewed phantasm of peace received again the desire that sprang in the heart of its father and lover, and throve and grew beautiful on it. Her terrible and infinite senility receded; Lawrence Wentworth's strong deceit forbade her to pass on to death and recalled her to apparent life. The suicide in the body had lost the vision of his destruction; the suicide in the soul had not yet reached his own. The thing became lovely with Adela's youth, and its lover slept.

In the morning, however, alone as usual, Wentworth was less at peace than had been his wont since the thing had come to him. In those earlier hours the night and his nightly companion were always indistinct. He preferred that indistinctness; he preferred, in the bright July mornings, to think of his work—the books he was reading, the book he was writing. He remembered that he had still a letter to write against Aston Moffatt, and had already begun it. But though he thought about his next unwritten sentence he could not ever manage to write it down. He would often go to his study in his dressing gown to get his papers, refusing to remember why they were not, as in the old days they used to be, lying by his bedside, or remembering only that it was because of the pleasant fantasies of his brain. So long as he could, in those early hours, pretend that it was only a mental fantasy he felt happier; he did not, just for those hours, quite like to admit that it was physical, because its actuality would have seemed in some way more immoral than a mental indulgence. His mind was certainly losing power. Afterwards as the day grew on, and the strength of his masculinity returned and swelled in him, he came to repose on his knowledge of its actual presence. But that morning he was troubled; he felt obscurely that something was attacking his peace. He moved restlessly; he got up and walked about; he tried to find refuge in this or the other thought; he failed. He would not go out that day; he sat about the house. And as the day went on he became aware that he feared to go out lest he should meet Adela Hunt, the real Adela Hunt on some real errand. He could not bear that; he could not bear her. What right had she to make his beloved a false image of her? It was after a solitary lunch and a fretful hour of work that he allowed himself at last to long for the succubus by day, and by day, knocking at his door—and he guessed who knocked and hurried himself to open it—it came. It sat in his room, and talked to him, with his own borrowed intelligence. It spoke of Cæsar and Napoleon, of generals and campaigns—traditions it could not know, history it could not recall, humanity it could not share. And still, though he was less unhappy, he was unhappy, for all that day, till the sun began to go down, he was haunted by a memory of another Adela. Even when his hand was on her bare arm, or hers caressing his, he was dimly troubled. He wanted to pull the curtains, to lock the doors, to bar out what was in his brain by barring his house, to be with what was irreconcilably not the world. He wanted either to shut himself wholly away from the world in a sepulchre of desire and satiety and renewed desire; or to destroy, if not the world, at least one form that walked in the world.

His trouble was increased by the likelihood of the intrusion of the world of the other Adela. He had, weeks since, sent to Mrs. Parry drawings and descriptions for the Grand Ducal uniforms. She had rung him up once or twice about them, and she was beginning to insist on his going round to her house to approve the result. He did not want to go to her house. He would be expected to be at the play, the performance of which was approaching, and he did not want to be at the play. Adela would be acting, and he didn't want to see her in her eighteenth-century costume, or any more at all. He would have to speak to her and he did not want to speak to her. He wanted to be alone with his fantasies. It was all the busy world, with Adela as its chief, that still hampered him. He could, of course, shut himself away, but if he were to enjoy the phantasm of Adela as he wanted to, his servants must see her and bring her tea and accept her as a visitor, and then what would they think if they heard of the actual Adela being seen somewhere else at the same time? Or if, by chance, the actual Adela should call?

It knew, with that accuracy with which it always prevented his desires, that he was disturbed about something it could not, until night came, cure. It spent on him a lingering gaze of love, and said: "I must go." It caught and kissed his hand in a hungry fire, and it looked up at him fervently and said: "To-night? Dear Lawrence, to-night?" He said "To-night", and desired to add the name. But he had never yet been able to do so—as if the name were indeed something actual, sacramental of reality. He said "To-night", and pressed it and kissed it and took it to the door, which he shut quickly, as he always did, for he had an uneasy wonder whether it ever went anywhere, once it had parted from him, and he did not wish to see it fade before his eyes into the air which, this summer, was growing so intolerably bright.

# Dress Rehearsal

The unusual brightness had been generally noticed. It was not a heat-wave; the weather was too gay and airy for that. It was an increase in luminous power; forms stood out more sharply, voices were heard more clearly. There seemed to be a heightening of capacity, within and without. The rehearsals of the play increased in effect, a kind of swiftness moved in the air; all things hastened. People said: "What a beautiful summer!" and went on saying it. One afternoon Pauline heard Stanhope, who had replied to that phrase a score of times, vary the reply by saying with some surprise: "O, the summer, do you think?" But his interlocutor had already been wafted away.

It was two days since the promise of substituted love, and it was their first meeting. She took advantage of her precursor's remark to say, as she shook hands, and their glances exchanged affection: "What then, if it isn't the summer?"

He shrugged delicately. "Only, does it seem like the summer?" he asked.

"Not very," she said. "But what do you think?"

"The air within the air, perhaps," he answered, half-serious. "The thing that increases everything that is, and decreases everything that isn't."

Pauline said, not upon any impulse of conventional chatter, "And which am I?"

"O *is*," he said, "*is*, decidedly. Unfortunately, perhaps, in many ways, but final. You haven't had any meetings yet?"

She began to answer and was cut short by new arrivals. It was the day of the dress rehearsal, and even the sophisticated practitioners of Battle Hill felt a new excitement.

Climax was at hand. The young and more innocent actors triumphed in a delight modified by fear of their incapacity; the more experienced feared the incapacity of others. Adela Hunt, for instance, was anxious that Periel and the Chorus should be her adequate background, and that her dramatic

137

lover should adore her urgently. He, a nice boy and shy, was too conscious of the Chorus individually to rise quite to the height of them in a mass. His voice still faltered with the smallest vibration of awareness upon the invocation of the fire. Mrs. Parry had pointed out to him that he must be used to burning leaves, and he had agreed; still, at the height of the verse, he trembled a little with the stress. The Bear, on the other hand, was distracted between his own wish to be ursine and Mrs. Parry's to be period. His two great moments, however, were in action rather than speech. One was a heavy pursuit of the Princess; at the other he and Periel intertwined in a dance among all the personages, drawing them into a complexity of union. He was not a pantomime bear; no assistant completed quadrupedicity; he walked bowed but upright, a bear's head, high furred boots, furred coat and gauntlets, making up the design which signified or symbolized the growling mass of animal life. Nor, though he and the spirit of the spirits danced together, did they ever meet or speak; between them always moved the mortal figures and harmonized their incommunicable utterances.

It was the reputation of Peter Stanhope which had so largely increased the excitement of this year's drama. Public attention was given to it; articles appeared in New York and paragraphs in Paris. Seats had to be reserved for a few—a very few— very distinguished visitors; many others could be and had to be refused. The Press would be there. A palpitation of publicity went through the cast; the world seemed to flow towards Battle Hill. There was no denying that it was an event, almost a moment in the history of the imagination; recognized as such by, at least, a not inconsiderable minority of those who cared for such things, and a quite inconsiderable minority of those who did not, but who read everything in their papers. Even the cast were provided with tickets; and the rehearsal itself was guarded by a policeman. A popular member of the Chorus also stood by the gate and scrutinized all arrivals, as if the bear and the spirit purged creation by power and knowledge.

The pressure of this outer world had modulated and unified the producer, the performers, and every one else concerned with the play. Harmony became so necessary that it was actually achieved, fate and free-will coinciding. Stanhope became so desirable that he was compelled to promise to say a few words at the end. A deference towards him exhibited itself. Adela rebuked Pauline for speaking lightly of the great man.

"I didn't know that you admired him so much yourself," Pauline said.

Adela, with an unfailing grasp of the real values of the world, said: "Even if I didn't, he is respected by some very fine judges. But I've come to see there is more in him than I'd thought. He's got a number of curiously modern streaks under his romanticism."

When Adela mentioned romanticism Pauline, and most other people, changed the conversation. Otherwise it was a prelude to a long and complete denunciation of all romantics as the enemies of true art. True art had been recently defined, by a distinguished critic, as "the factual oblique", and of the factual oblique romanticism, it seemed, was incapable, being neither clear enough to be factual or clever enough to be oblique. The factual oblique, incidentally, had not yet revealed to Adela the oblique fact that she never mentioned romanticism when she was with Hugh; any conversation in which it seemed likely to appear was deflected before it arrived. Pauline, not having been able to deflect, merely altered.

"There's Mr. Wentworth," she said. "I do hope he approves of the Guard."

"He ought to have looked at them before," Adela said severely. "He's been terribly slack. I suppose you haven't seen him lately?"

"No, not with grandmother and the play and everything," Pauline answered. "Have you?"

Adela shook her head. Wentworth was moving slowly across the lawn towards them. His eyes were on the ground; he walked heavily, and it was as if by accident that he at last drew level with them. Pauline said: "Good afternoon, Mr. Wentworth."

He looked up at her, and blinked. It was true the air was very clear and the sun very bright, yet Pauline was astonished by the momentary difficulty he seemed to find in focusing her. When he had got her right, he slowly smiled, and said: "Ah! Good afternoon, Miss Anstruther."

Adela Hunt abruptly said: "Mr. Wentworth!" He jumped. Slightly but definitely he jerked, and only then looked round. He looked, and there was perplexity in his eyes. He stared at the surprised Adela; he seemed taken aback at seeing her, and almost to resent it. A disagreeable shock showed in his face, and was gone, as he answered: "Oh, yes; Miss Hunt", a statement, not a greeting: a piece of information offered to the inquiring mind. Adela could not help noticing it, and was almost too astonished to smile. She couldn't believe the look had been acted, yet he couldn't really be surprised. She wondered if he were indeed secretly angry, if it were a poor mad insult of an outraged mind, and decided it couldn't be.

She said briskly: "I hope you've approved of the uniforms." He took a step back. He said, in real distress: "Oh, hush, hush, not so loud," and in turn he blinked at her, as if, when he had taken in her words, they surprised him more. Little though she could know it, they did. He had supposed, in the night and the morning, that he had hated the Adela of the world; he had had her in his imagination as an enemy and a threat. He had overrated her. She was, in fact, nothing like what he had, and now he had met her he had hardly recognized her. There had been a girl talking to—to—the name had again escaped him—to the other girl, whose shape had reminded him of his nightly mistress; she had turned her head, and it had been his mistress, and then again it was not. It could not be, for this one was remote and a little hostile; it was not, for this one was nothing like as delightful, as warm, as close-bewildering. She spoke, and it was strange, for he expected love; he did not want that voice except in love, and now it— at first—said strange things. With relief he realized it was not *his* voice—so he called it, admirably exact; this was not the voice of *his* mistress, and his mistress was most particularly he. This distressed him; it was loud, harsh, uncouth. It was like the rest of the tiresome world into which he had been com- pelled to enter—violent, smashing, bewildering by its harsh clamour, and far from the soft sweetness of his unheard melody. It was not without reason that Keats imagined the lover of unheard melody in reverie on stone images; the real Greek dancers would have pleased him less. But though Went- worth was shocked by the clumsy tread and the loud voice, they relieved him also. He had hated once; but then he had not wanted to hate—it disturbed him too much; and now he knew he did not. He need not resent the grossness of the world; enough if, by flight, he rejected it. He had his own living medicament for all trouble, and distaste and oblivion for everything else—most of all for his noisome parody of his peace.

Adela said, modulating her voice: "Have you got a head- ache? what a shame! it's good of you to turn out, but we do want to be sure everything's all right. I mean, if we must have uniforms. Personally . . ."

Wentworth said, in a voice of exhaustion: "Oh, please!" In this stridency, as it seemed to him, there was a suggestion of another disastrous noise—the nightmare of a groan, tearing up the abyss, setting the rope swinging. The dull, heavy, plain thing opposite him became identified to his pained sense with that dreadful break-up of his dream, and now he could not hide. He could not say to the hills of those comforting breasts: "Cover me". The sound sang to his excruciated body, as the sight oppressed it. The two imprisoned and split him: they held him and searched his entrails. They *wanted* something of him. He refused to want anything but what he wanted.

While Adela stared, half offended by his curious moan, he withdrew himself into his recesses, and refused to be wanted. Like the dead man on his flight down the hill, he declined communion. But he, to whom more room and beauty in life had been given, chances of clarity and devotion, was not now made frightening to himself. He had not known fear, nor did he find fear, nor was fear the instrument of salvation. He had what he had. There were presented to him the uniforms of the Grand Ducal Guard.

A voice as loud but less devastating than Adela's, for it recalled no unheard melodies, said behind him: "Mr. Wentworth! at last! we're all ready for you. Pauline, the Guard are over by the beeches: take Mr. Wentworth across. I'll be there in a minute." Mrs. Parry, having said this, did not trouble to watch them do it. She went on.

Pauline smiled at Wentworth's dazed and Adela's irritated face. She said: "I suppose we'd better. Would you, Mr. Wentworth?"

He turned to her with relief. The sound of her voice was quieter than the rest. He had never before thought so, but now certainly it was. He said, "Yes, yes; let's get away."

Pauline saw Adela as they turned from her, a Gorgon of incredulity. Her heart laughed, and they went. As they passed over the grass, she said: "I do hope you haven't a headache? They're so trying."

He answered, a little relieved to be away from the dull shouting oppression of Adela: "People are so noisy. Of course . . . anything I can do . . . but I can't stop long."

"I shouldn't think it would take more than a few minutes," Pauline said. "You'll only have to say yes or no—practically. And," she added, looking round at the whole chaos of glory, and instinctively discerning Stanhope in the distance, "as it's too late for anything else, you might be so very kind as to enjoy us for what we are, and say yes."

Hugh Prescott, grand-ducally splendid and dramatically middle-aged, ran after them. He said, as he caught them up: "Hallo, Mr. Wentworth! I hope my Guard'll be correct."

Wentworth had been soothed by Pauline's voice. It had to his mind, after Adela's, something of that quality he desired. It mingled with him; it attracted him; it carried him almost to that moment he knew so well, when, as the desire that expressed his need awoke and grew in him, there came a point of abandonment to his desire. He did not exactly will, but he refused to avoid. Why, indeed, he had once asked himself, swiftly, almost thoughtlessly, should he avoid? He asked himself no more; he sighed, and as it were, nestled back into himself, and then it would somehow be there—coming from behind, or speaking in his ear, or perhaps not even that, but a breath mingling with his, almost dividing from his to mingle with it, so that there were two where there had been one, and then the breath seemed to wander away into his palm where his hand lay half-closed, and became a hand in his own hand, and then a slow arm grew against his, and so, a tender coil against him or a swift energy of hunger, as his mood was, it was there, and when the form was felt, it could at last be seen, and he sank into its deep inviting eyes. As he listened to Pauline he suddenly knew all this, as he had never known it before; he almost saw it happen as a thing presented. Her voice created, but it separated. It brought him almost to his moment, and coiled away, with him in its toils. It directed him to the Guard; it said, with an intensity that Pauline had never uttered, but he in his crisis heard: "Take us as we are, and say yes; say yes or no . . . we are . . . we are . . . say yes . . .", and another voice, "Is the Grand Duke's Guard correct?" They became, as he paused before the displayed magnificence, a chorus swinging and singing: "We are . . . we are . . . we

are. . . . Is the Guard correct? . . . Say, say, O say . . . is the
Guard, is the Guard correct?"

It was not. In one flash he saw it. In spite of his diagrams
and descriptions, they had got the shoulder-knots all wrong.
The eighteenth century had never known that sort of thing.
He looked at them, for the first moment almost with the pure
satisfaction of the specialist. He almost, somewhere in him,
joined in that insane jangle: "No, no, no; the Guard is wrong
—O, wrong. Say . . . I say. . . ." He looked, and he swung, as
if on his rope, as if at a point of decision—to go on or to
climb up. He walked slowly along the line, round the back,
negligent of remarks and questions, outwardly gazing, in-
wardly swinging. After that first glance, he saw nothing else
clearly. "Say yes or no. . . ." The shoulder-knots could be
altered easily enough, all twelve, in an hour or so's work. Or
pass them—"take us as we are . . . say yes." They could be
defended, then and there, with half a dozen reasons; they
were no more of a jumble than Stanhope's verse. But he was
something of a purist; he did not like them. His housekeeper,
for that matter, could alter them that evening under his
direction, and save the costume-makers any further trouble.
"Is the Guard, is the Grand Duke's Guard, correct?"

A voice penetrated him. Hugh was saying: "One must
have one's subordinates exact, mustn't one?" There was the
slightest stress on "subordinates"—or was there? Wentworth
looked askance at him; he was strolling superb by his side.
Pauline said: "We could alter some things, of course." His
silence had made her anxious. He stood away, and surveyed
the backs of the Guard. He could, if he chose, satisfy and complete everything. He could have the coats left at his house
after the rehearsal; he could do what the honour of his scholarship commanded; he could have them returned. It meant
only his being busy with them that one evening, and concerning himself with something different from his closed garden.
He smelt the garden.

# Dress Rehearsal

Mrs. Parry's voice said: "Is the Guard correct?" He said: "Yes." It was over; he could go.

He had decided. The jingle was in his ears no more. Everything was quite quiet. The very colours were still. Then from a distance movement began again. His future was secure, both proximate and ultimate. But his present was decided for him; he was not allowed to go. The devil, for that afternoon, promptly swindled him. He had cheated; he was at once cheated. Mrs. Parry expected him to stop for the rehearsal and oversee the movement of the Guard wherever, in its odd progress about the play, it marched on or marched off. She made it clear. He chattered a protest, to which she paid no attention. She took him to a chair, saw him in it, and went off. He had no energy to oppose her. No one had. Over all that field of actors and spectators—over Stanhope and Pauline, over Adela and Hugh, over poetry and possession and sacred possession the capacity of one really capable woman imposed itself. The moment was hers, and in view of her determination the moment became itself. As efficient in her kind as Margaret Anstruther in hers, Catherine Parry mastered creation, and told it what to do. She had taken on her job, and the determination to fulfil her job controlled the utterance of the poetry of Stanhope and delayed the operation of the drugs of Lilith. Wentworth struggled and was defeated, Adela writhed but obeyed, Peter Stanhope laughed and enjoyed and assented. It was not perhaps the least achievement of his art that it had given to his personal spirit the willingness to fulfil the moment as the moment, so that, reserving his own apprehension of all that his own particular business meant to him, he willingly subordinated it to the business of others at their proper time. He seconded Mrs. Parry as far as and in every way that he could. He ran errands, he took messages, he rehearsed odd speeches, he fastened hooks and held weapons. But he only seconded her. The efficiency was hers; and the Kingdom of God which fulfilled itself in the remote recesses of his spacious verse fulfilled itself also in her effective supremacy. She stood in the middle of the field and looked around her. The few spectators were seated; the actors were gathering. Stanhope stood by her side. The Prologue, with his trumpet, ran hastily across the stage to the trees which formed the background. Mrs. Parry said: "I think we're ready?" Stanhope agreed. They retired to their chairs, and Mrs. Parry nodded vigorously to the Prologue. The rehearsal began.

Wentworth, sitting near to Stanhope, secluded himself from it as much as possible, reaching backward and forward with closed eyes into his own secrecies. At the extreme other end of activity, Pauline, waiting with the Chorus for the Woodcutter's Son's speech, upon which, as he fed the flames, the first omnipotent song was to break, also gave herself up to delight. If the heavens had opened, it was not for her to deny them, or even too closely to question or examine them. She carried, in her degree, Peter Stanhope and his fortunes—not for audience or other publicity but for the achievement of the verse and the play itself. It was all very well for Stanhope to say it was an entertainment and not a play, and to be charmingly and happily altruistic about her, and since he preferred her to fall in with Mrs. Parry's instructions she did it, for everyone's sake including her own. But he was used, anyhow in his imagination, to greater things; this was the greatest she had known or perhaps was ever likely to know. If the apparition she had so long dreaded came across the field she would look at it with joy. If it would sit down till the rehearsal was over. . . . She smiled to herself at the fantasy and laughed to think that she could smile. The Woodcutter's Son from beside her went forward, carrying his burden of twigs. His voice rose in the sublime speculations of fire and glory which the poet's reckless generosity had given him. He spoke and paused, and Pauline and all the Chorus, moving so that their own verdure showed among the trees, broke into an answering song.

# Dress Rehearsal

She was not aware, as the rehearsal proceeded, of any other sensation than delight. But so clear and simple was that delight, and so exquisitely shared by all the performers in their separate ways, that as between the acts they talked and laughed together, and every one in the field, with the exception of Lawrence Wentworth, joined in that universal joy—so single and fundamental did it become that once, while again she waited, it seemed to her as if the very words "dress rehearsal" took on another meaning. She saw the ceremonial dress of the actors, but it did not seem to her stranger than Mrs. Parry's frock or Stanhope's light suit. All things at all times and everywhere, rehearsed; some great art was in practice and the only business anyone had was to see that his part was perfect. And this particular rehearsal mirrored the rest—only that this was already perfected from within, and that other was not yet. The lumbering Bear danced; the Grand Duke uttered his gnomic wisdom; the Princess and the Woodcutter's Son entered into the lucid beauty of first love; the farmers counted their pence; and the bandits fell apart within.

It was in the pause before the last act that the dark thought came to her. She had walked a little away from the others to rest her soul, and, turning, looked back. Around the place where lately the fire had burned, the Prologue and some of the Guard were talking. She saw him lift his trumpet; she saw them move, and the uniforms shone in the amazing brightness of the sun, and suddenly there came to her mind another picture; the woodcut in the old edition of the *Book of Martyrs*. There too was a trumpet, and guards, and a fire, and a man in it. Here, the tale said, and she had not remembered it till now, here where this stage, perhaps where this fire lay, they had done him to death by fire.

She had had the last act in mind as she turned, the act in which physical sensation, which is the play of love, and pardon, which is the speed of love, and action, which is the fact of love, and almighty love itself, all danced together; and

147

now a shadow lay across it, the shadow of death and cruelty, the living death. The sun was still bright, colours vivid, laughter gay, and the shadow was the centre of them all. The shadow was a hollow, filled with another, quite different, fact. She felt the pang of the last hopelessness. If the living who walked in the gutters of mind or spirit, if the present misery of the world, were healed, or could be forgotten, still there sprang out of the hollow the knowledge of the dead whose unrecompensed lives had gone before that joy. The past accused her, made terrible by the certain history of her house. His blood was in her and made demands on hers. He had gone willingly to death, chosen it, insisted on it; his judges had been willing enough to spare him if he would commit himself to a phrase or two. But still in the end they had inflicted death, and agony in death; and the world that had inflicted and enjoyed and nourished itself on agony was too like the world in which she moved, too like Hugh and Adela and Catherine Parry and the rest. She had been lost in a high marvel, but if that joy were seriously to live it must somehow be reconciled with the agony that had been; unless hollow and shell were one, there was only hollow and shell.

She walked back, and as she did so Stanhope saw her and came across.

"Well," he said, "it all seems going very well."

She said, with a coldness in her voice that rose from the creeping hollow of the darkness. "You think so? . . . did you know an ancestor of mine was burnt alive just here?"

He turned to walk by her. "I did," he said. "I'd read it, of course—after all, it's my house—and your grandmother spoke of it."

She said: "Well?" and then repentantly, "I'm sorry but . . . we're all so happy. The play, the fire—*our* fire, it's all so wonderful. And yet we can do *that*. How can we be happy, unless we forget? and how can we forget? how can we dare forget?"

148

He said: "Forget nothing. Unless everything's justifiable, nothing is. But don't you forget, perhaps, something else?"

She looked at him with question. He went on: "Mightn't his burden be carried too?"

She stopped; she said staring: "But he's dead!"

"And so?" Stanhope asked mildly, and waited.

She said: "You mean . . . you can't mean . . . ?" As her voice hung baffled, there arose gigantic before her the edge of a world of such incredible dimensions that she was breathless at the faint hint. Her mouth opened; her eyes stared. Her head was spinning. She said: "But. . . ."

Stanhope took her arm to propel her gently forward; then, letting it go, he said: "A good deal of our conversation consists of saying *but* to each other. However, who shall fail to follow when . . . and so forth. 'But—' Periel?"

"But he's dead," she repeated. It was not what she meant to say.

"So you remarked," Stanhope said gently. "And I asked you what that had to do with it. Or words to that effect. You might as well say he had red hair, as for all I know he may have had. Yes, yes, Mrs. Parry."

He raised his voice and waved back. "We shall be delaying the rehearsal," he said. "Come along—all things in their order."

She asked, inadvertently, as she quickened her steps to keep pace with him: "Do you tell me to try and carry *his* fear?"

"Well," he answered, "you can't make contract; so far, it's true, death or red hair or what not interferes. But you might, in the Omnipotence, offer him your—anything you've got. Only I should intend to have it first."

"Intend to have it?" she asked breathlessly.

"Intend to have joy to offer," he said. "Be happy—take all the happiness, if it's there, that you may not offer the Lord what costs nothing. You must have a small private income to try and help support even a Marian martyr. Heavens, they *are* waiting. To your tent, O Periel." As she ran he exclaimed after her. "Perhaps that's the difference between Israel and Judah! they went to their own tents and left David to his. Hence the Dispersion . . . and the Disappearance."

"What disappearance, Mr. Stanhope?" Mrs. Parry asked.

He had come level with her while he was still speaking, and he made a small gesture. "Nothing, Mrs. Parry. Of the saviour of his own life. How well this act opens, doesn't it?"

As Pauline, escaping Mrs. Parry's eye, ran across the stage, and threaded her way between the persons to her position, her mind was more breathless than she. She felt again, as in a low but immense arc rising above the horizon of her world, or perhaps of the earth itself, the hint of a new organization of all things: a shape, of incredible difficulty in the finding, of incredible simplicity found, an infinitely alien arrangement of infinitely familiar things. The bottom had dropped out of her universe, yet her astonished spirit floated and did not fall. She was a little sick with running, running into this other world. She halted, turned, addressed herself. She turned to the play where martyrdom had been—to the martyrdom. "I have seen the salvation of my God." The salvation throbbed in the air above her; it thrilled in the mortal light. " 'Unto him that hath shall be given' . . . 'what of him that hath not?' " A voice, neither of the martyr nor his executioner, answered, singing, with a terrible clarity of assured fact—fact, the only thing that can be loved: "from him that hath not shall be taken away even that which he seemeth to have". A trumpet was crying, crying for the execution of the justice of the Queen's Majesty on a convicted and impenitent heretic. His blood was in her veins; dazed with her own will, she struggled to pay the dues of her inheritance. The sudden crowd of adorned figures thronged before her. He was not there; he was dead centuries since. If centuries meant anything; perhaps they didn't—perhaps everything was all at once, and interchanged devotion; perhaps even now he burned, and she and her friends danced, and her grandmother died and lived, and Peter Stanhope wrote his verse, and all the past of the Hill was one with its present. It lived; it intermingled; not among these living alone did the doctrine of substituted love bear rule. Her intention rose, and was clear, and withdrew, as the stage opened for her advance About her the familiar and transfigured personages moved; this was the condition and this the air of supernatural life. *Ecce, omnia nova facio.* The incantation and adoration of the true substance of experience sounded. She fulfilled her part in a grave joy, aspiring to become part of that substance. All drew to its close; the dress rehearsal ended. Remained only the performance of the play.

## Chapter Nine

# THE TRYST OF THE WORLDS

As if the world of that other life to which this in which Margaret Anstruther lay was but spectral, and it to this, renewed itself with all its force in the groan he heard, as if that groan had been but its own energy of freeing itself, the dead man found when it ceased that he was standing alone among the houses. He remembered the vanished apparitions clearly enough, two images of beauty. He had seen an old woman and a young, though the younger form had been faint with distance. The colour which she hinted was obscured; in the older there was no colour but softness of light. Now he was in the street. His back was to the house. He was looking along the road, and he saw, beyond it at the point where the light of the sun, whatever sun, lay halted, the house and the ladder he knew. He saw the light beyond it, softer than before, as it were of one kind with that of the woman with whom he had spoken. The house itself was dark; the ladder was white with a bony pallor against it, but it held no sun. There it stood, waiting for him to go back.

There had been an opening up within him. He had run in his life after other men, and in his second life away from other selves. His unapt mind had been little use to him. It had been trying to please others or himself, naturally and for long properly. He was relieved of this necessity. There was only one way to go, and the only question if he should go. He could move, or not. He knew this, yet, like Pauline when she kept her promise to Stanhope, he knew that he had already chosen, had come into obedience, and was no longer free. He began to walk. He had not realized that the choice was there until the choice had been made. Wentworth, turning from the Grand Ducal Guard, did not realize it even then; as Macbeth did not know he had accepted his deed when he accepted the means, and conceded his sin to his conviction of success.

In effect, the dead man's choice, like all choices of the kind, had been less than it seemed. He could go, or he could wait till he was driven. In the hastening or delaying of the end lies all distinction in the knowledge of the end when at last it comes. At rare moments speed is determined; all else is something else. He went, and with more energy than he had ever known. The lost power of his missed youth awoke in him, and of his defrauded manhood. It was needed. He had not taken a dozen steps before the memory of his latest experience became as faint as the old woman's voice had been. He did not again feel his old fear, but he was intensely aware of ignorance. There were now no shapes. He was alone, and the pallid ladder of the dark house stood before him. The light beyond was soft, but promised nothing. As he went soundlessly he had no thought but that it was better to do at once what must be done, and that he had seen, if only in a fading apparition, the tender eyes of love.

He passed the finished houses; he came among those which, by the past or future, had been unbuilt. As he reached them he heard a faint sound. He had come again into the peculiar territory of the dead. He heard behind him a small rustle, as if of dead leaves or snakes creeping out from dry sticks. He did not think of snakes or leaves, nor of the dead leaves of a great forest, the still-existent nothingness of life. Those who had known the green trees were tangled and torn in the dry. The tragedies of Peter Stanhope carried the image of that pain-piercing nothing. The dead man, like Pauline, had lived with thorns and hard wood, and at last they had destroyed him as pitilessly as the Marian martyr. He did not therefore conceive them now as anything but a mere sound. It went with him along the road. and when he had come fully out at the end into the space where the ladder of bone led again to a darkness of the grave, it had become louder. He heard it on all sides. He stopped and turned.

The shapes were standing in a great crowd watching him. Mostly they had his form and face, and they stood, in the infinite division of past moments, but higgledy-piggledy, sombrely staring. He saw in front, parodying earthly crowds, the children—different ages, different sizes, all looking with his small pointed hungry face. In the massed multitude behind there were, at points, different faces, faces of any few creatures who for one reason or another had mattered to his mind. He saw his wife in several places; he saw the face of a youth who had been the nearest he had known to a friend; he saw those he had disliked. But, at most, these others were few.

The crowd did not move, except that sometimes other single forms slipped out of the ruined houses, swelling it as crowds are swelled in London streets. It was useless, had he desired it, to attempt to return. He turned away from them again, but this time not merely from them but towards something, towards the ladder. He laid a hand on it. The long hard dry rustle came again, as the whole crowd fell forward, bones shifting and slipping as some moving vitality slid through them. They closed towards him, their thronged circles twisting round the house and him as if they were the snake. His mortal mind would have given way, could it have apprehended such a strait between shadowy bone and shining bone; his immortal, nourished by belief in the mother of his soul, remained clear. His seeming body remained capable. He exercised his choice, and began to go up the ladder. At once, with a horrid outbreak of shifting leaves and snapping sticks and rustling bodies, they were about its foot, looking up. The living death crowded round the ladder of bone, which it could not ascend. White faces of unvitalized, unsubstantial, yet real, existence, looked up at him mounting. Nothingness stared and panted, with false breath, terrible to those who live of choice in its phantasmal world. But for him, who rose above them to that stage set in the sky, the expanded point and culminating area of his last critical act, the place of skull and consciousness, of life and death and life, for him there entered through the grasp he had on the ladder shafts an energy. He looked neither down nor up; he went on. A wind had risen about him, as if here the movement of the leaves, if leaves, shook the air, and not the air the leaves. It was as if a last invisible tentacle were sent up by the nothingness to draw him back into the smooth undulations below, that its sterility might bury him in a living sepulchre; the identities of the grave moving in a blind instinct to overtake and seize him. Now and then some of them even began to mount a few rungs, but they could get and keep no hold. They fell again to their own level.

He did not see this, for his eyes were above. In the same sense of nothing but action he climbed the last rungs, and stood on the stage from which he had been flung. But he had hardly stepped on to it before it changed. He had come back from his own manner of time to the point in the general world of time from which he had fled, and he found it altered. The point of his return was not determined by himself, but by his salvation, by a direction not yet formulated, by the economy of means of the Omnipotence, by the moment of the death of Margaret Anstruther. Therefore he came into the built house, and the room where Wentworth slept. The open stage closed round him as he came upon it. The walls rose; there was a ceiling above. He knew he stood in a room, though the details were vague. It was ghostly to him, like that other in which, a short time before, he had stood. There the old woman had been a vivid centre to him. Here he was not, at first, aware of a centre. In this other world he had not been astonished at the manner in which things happened, but now he was a little uncomfortable. He thought at first it was because he could have had no business in such a room during his earlier life. So perhaps it was, but if so, another cause had aroused the old uneasiness—the faint hint of a slither of dry leaves, such as he had heard behind him along the road, but now within the room. It displeased and diseased him; he must remove himself. It was almost his first quiet decision ever; he was on the point to enter into actions of peace. The courtesy that rules the world of spirits took him, and as the creature that lay in the room had not entered except under Wentworth's compulsion, so this other made haste to withdraw from its intrusion. Also he was aware that, having re-entered this place and point of time, this station of an inhabited world, by the ladder of bone from the other side, he must go now farther on the way. He had the City in his mind; he had his wife in mind. He could not tell by what means or in what shape he would find her, or if he would find her. But she was his chief point of knowledge, and to that he directed himself. Of the necessity of getting a living he did not think. Living, whether he liked it or not, was provided; he knew that he did like. He went carefully across the dim room and through the door; down the stairs, and reached the front door. It opened of itself before him, so he thought, and he peered out into the road. A great blackness was there; it changed as he peered. As if it fled from him, it retreated. He heard the wind again, but now blowing up the street. A shaft of light smote along with it. Before wind and light and himself he saw the night turn, but it was not the mere night; it was alive, it was made of moving and twisting shapes hurrying away of their own will. Light did not drive them; they revealed the light as they went. They rose and rushed; as they disappeared he saw the long drive before him, and at its end, in the street proper, the figure of a girl.

In a different darkness, mortally illumined, Pauline, not far away, had that previous evening been sitting by her grandmother's bed. It was, to her, the night after the rehearsal. She had come home to find Margaret awake, alert, inquiring, and after she had spoken of the details of the afternoon, she had not been able, nor wished, to keep from speaking of the other thing that filled and threatened her mind. Her grandmother's attention still seemed to her acute, even if remote. Indeed, all mortal things were now remote to Margaret unless they were vividly consistent with the slope over which she moved. She felt, at intervals, someone being lifted and fed, someone hearing and speaking intelligible words. Only sometimes did definiteness from that other casual state enter her; then she and it were sharply present. For the rest she only saw vague images of a great good, and they faded, and at rarer intervals in the other single consciousness of slow—but slow!—movement over a surface, an intense sweetness pierced her. She moaned then, for it was pain; she moaned happily, for it was only the last inevitable sloth of her body that made its pain, resisting, beyond her will, the translucent energy. She always assented. She assented now to what Pauline was saying, sitting by her bed, her fingers interlocked and pressed against her knee, her body leaning forward, her breath drawn with a kind of slow difficulty against the beating passion of her heart's presagements. She was saying: "But how could one give backwards?"

Margaret could not, at that point of experience, explain metaphysics. She said: "If it's like that, my dear?"

Pauline said: "But if he took it? I thought—there—I might: but now, I daren't."

She saw Margaret's smile flash at her across rocks. It went and the voice said: "You think it's yours?"

Pauline answered, abruptly checking abruptness: "I don't. . . . Do I?"

"You think one of the two's yours—joy or misery," Margaret said, "or both. Why, if you don't, should you mind?"

Pauline for a minute struggled with this in silence: then, evading it, she returned to time. "But four hundred years," she exclaimed.

"Child," her grandmother said, "I can touch Adam with my hand; you aren't as far off."

"But how could he take it before I'd given it?" Pauline cried, and Margaret said: "Why do you talk of *before?* If you give, you give to It, and what does It care about *before?*"

Pauline got up and walked to the window. It was drawing towards night, yet so translucent was the pale green sky that night and day seemed alike unthinkable. She heard in the distance a single pair of hurrying feet; patter, patter. She said, in a muffled voice: "Even the edge frightens me."

"Peter Stanhope," Margaret said, "must have been frightened many times."

"O—poetry!" Pauline exclaimed bitterly. "That's different; you know it is, grandmother."

"In seeing?" Margaret asked. "And as for being, you must find out for yourself. He can carry your parcels, but not you."

"Couldn't he?" Pauline said. "Not that I want him to."

"Perhaps," Margaret answered. "But I think only when you don't need it, and your parcels when you do."

Her voice grew faint as she spoke, and Pauline came quickly back to the bed.

"I'm tiring you," she said hastily. "I'm sorry: look, I'll go now. I didn't mean to talk so much."

Margaret glanced at her, and said in a whisper: "But I'd so much rather die talking." All talk of the divine thing was pleasant to her, even if this beating of wings in the net, wings so dear and so close, was exhausting in the thin air. Pauline, looking down for a second after her good-night, thought that a change had taken place. The eyes had closed, though the girl was by no means sure that they were not as alert now as they had been when they were open and watching.

Yet a proportion between the old woman and external things had been withdrawn; another system of relations might have been established, but if so it was unapprehensible by others. But the change in customary relations was definitely apprehensible. She looked small, and yet small was hardly the word; she was different. The body had been affected by a change of direction in the spirit, and only when the spirit was removed would it regain for a little while its measurable place amongst measurable things. It could be served and aided; but the ceremonies of service were now made to something strange that existed among them. The strangeness communicated itself, by a kind of opposition, to the very bed in which that body was stretched; it became a mound of earth lifted up to bear the visiting victim. The woman who was their companion had half-changed into a visitor from another place, a visitor who knew nothing of the world to which she was still half-native. The unknown and the known mingled, as if those two great parents of humanity allowed their mingled powers to be evident to whoever watched. The mound, in the soft light of the room, presented itself to Pauline as if its low height was the crown and peak of a life; the long journey had ended on this cavity in the rounded summit of a hill. She considered it gravely so before she turned and, leaving the nurse in charge, went to her own room.

She was not asleep when later in the night she was called. Her grandmother, the nurse said, needed her. Pauline pulled a dressing-gown on her and went across. Mrs. Anstruther was sitting in the bed, propped by pillows; her eyes looking away out of the room. As if she dared not turn her gaze away, she said, as Pauline came up: "Is that you, darling?"

"Me," the girl answered. "Did you want me?"

"Will you do something for me?" Mrs. Anstruther said. "Something rather odd?"

"Why, of course," the girl said. "Anything. What is it?"

"Would you be so very charming as to go out and see if anyone wants you?" Mrs. Anstruther said, quite distinctly. "Up by Mr. Wentworth's."

"She's wandering," the nurse whispered. Pauline, used to Mrs. Anstruther's extremely unwandering habits, hesitated to agree. But it was certainly rather odd. She said, with a tenderness a little fractured by doubt, "Wants *me*, darling? Now?"

"Of course, *now*," her grandmother answered. "That's the point. I think perhaps he ought to get back to the City." She looked round with a little sigh. "Will you?"

Pauline had been about to make the usual unfelicitous efforts of the healthy to persuade the sick that they are being rightly served. But she could not do it. No principle and no wisdom directed her, nor any conscious thought of love. She merely could not do it. She said: "By Mr. Wentworth's? Very well, darling." She could have helped, but did not, adding: "I don't think it's very likely."

"No," said Margaret, and Pauline was gripped by a complete sense of folly. " 'I don't think it's . . . No.' " She said: "I don't know a thing. I'll go." And turned. The nurse said as she moved to the door: "Sweet of you to be so nice. Come back in ten minutes or so. She won't realize the time."

"I'm going," Pauline said, distantly, and distinctly, "as far as Mr. Wentworth's. I shall be as quick as I can." She saw a protest at the nurse's mouth, and added: "At once."

She dressed quickly. Even so, in spite of her brave words to the nurse, her doubts were quicker. In spite of her intention, she reasoned against her promise. Three words dogmatized definition at her: "Her mind's wandering; her mind's wandering." Why, obeying that wandering mind, should she herself wander on the Hill? Why, in a lonely street, under the pale shining sky, should she risk the last dreadful meeting? The high clock struck one; time drew to the night's nadir. Why go? why go? Sit here, she said, almost aloud, and say "Peace". Is it peace, Jehu? cry peace where there is no peace; *faciunt solitudinem et pacem vocant*. She would make a solitude round the dying woman and call it peace; the dying woman would die and never know, or dying know and call it well; the dying woman that would not die but see, or die and see; and dead, see and know—know the solitude that her granddaughter had called peace. Up and up, the wind was rising, and the shuffle of leaves under the moon, and nothing was there for her to find, but to find nothing now was to be saved from finding nothing in the place where whatever she now did was hid and kept and saved. The edge of the other world was running up along the sky, the world where everyone carried themselves but everyone carried someone else's grief: Alice in Wonderland, sweet Alice, Alice sit by the fire, the fire burned: who sat by the fire that burned a man in another's blood on the grass of a poet's house, where things were given backward, and rules were against rights and rights against rules, and a ghost in the fire was a ghost in the street, and the thing that had been was the thing that was to be and it was coming, was coming; what was coming? what but herself? she was coming, she was coming, up the street and the wind; herself—a terrible good, terror and error, but the terror was error, and the error was in the terror, and now all were in him, for he had taken them into himself, and he was coming, down all the roads of Battle Hill, closing them in him, making them straight: make straight the highways before our God, and they were not for God took them, in the world that was running through this, its wheel turning within this world's air, rolling out of the air. No peace but peace, no joy but joy, no love but love. Behold, I come quickly. Amen, even so, come. . . .

She caught up a hat and flung herself at the door, her blood burning within her, as the house burned around. The air was fiery to her sense; she breathed a mingled life, as if the flames of poetry and martyrdom rose together in the air within the air, and touched the outer atmosphere with their interior force. She ran down the stairs, but already her excitement, being more excitement than strength, flagged and was pain. Action was not yet so united with reaction as to become passion. The doubt she must have of what was to come took its old habitual form. Her past pretended to rule her, *de facto* sovereign, and her past was fear. It was midnight, the Hill was empty, she was alone. It could only be that her ghostly image lay, now, in wait for her to emerge into its desolate kingdom. She grit her teeth. The thing must be done. She had promised her grandmother; more important still, she had promised the nurse. She might have confided to the first what she would never concede to the second. It was then that she saw the telephone.

At first, as she paused a minute in the hall, to settle herself— to settle her determination that that woman who had talked of wandering minds should not find her foolish expectation fulfilled—at first she did not think of Stanhope; then inevitably, with her grief stirring in her, she did. To think of him was to think, at once, of speaking to him. The telephone. She thought: "One o'clock and he's asleep; don't be a fool." She thought: " 'Any hour of the day or night'." She thought: "I oughtn't to disturb him," and then with the clarity of that world of perpetual exchange: "I ought to disturb him." It was her moral duty to wake him up, if he was asleep and she could. She smiled, standing in the hall where the new light of the summer sky dimly shone. Reversal had reached its extreme; she who had made a duty of her arrogance had found a duty in her need. Her need retreated beneath the shock. At precisely the moment when she could have done without him she went to ask for him; the glad and flagrant mockery of the Omnipotence lay peaceful in her heart as she dialled his number, her finger slowing a little on the last figure, as if the very notion were a delight too sweet to lose by haste. The receiver at her ear, as if she leant to it, she waited. Presently she heard his voice.

She said, again grave: "Are you awake enough to hear me?"

"Complete with attention," he answered. "Whatever it is, how very, very right of you! That's abstract, not personal. Concede the occasion."

# The Tryst of the Worlds

"The occasion," she said, "is that I'm going out up the Hill because my grandmother's asked me to, and I was a little afraid just now . . . I'm not."

"O blessed, blessed," Stanhope murmured, but whether he thought of her or the Omnipotence she did not know. He added, to her: "Go in peace. Would you like me to come?"

"No, of course not," she answered, and lingering still a minute said: "I thought I wanted to ring you up, but when I did I didn't. Forgive me."

"If it gives you any pleasure," he said, "but you might have needed forgiveness in fact if you hadn't. God's not mine. Pardon, Periel, like love, is only ours for fun: essentially we don't and can't. But you want to go. . . . You'll remember?"

"For ever," she said, "and ever and ever. Thank you." She put the receiver firmly down, opened the door, and went out into the street. The pure night received her. Darkness was thick round the houses, but the streets lay clear. She was aware, immediately, of some unusualness, and presently she knew what it was. She was used to shadows lying across the pavements, but now it was not so. On either side of the street they gathered and blocked and hid the buildings, climbing up them, creepers of night, almost in visible movement. Between those masses the roads lay like the gullies of a mountain down which an army might come—broad and empty, prepared for an army, passes already closed by scouts and outposts, and watched by the dazzling flashes which now and then and here and there lit the sky, as if silver machines of air above the world moved in escort of expected power. Apart from those momentary dazzling flashes light was diffused through the sky. She could see no moon, only once or twice in her walk, at some corner, between the cliffs of darkness, far away on the horizon, she half-thought she saw a star—Hesper or Phosphor, the planet that is both the end and the beginning, Venus, omega and alpha, transliteration of speech. Once, far behind her, she thought she heard hurrying footsteps, but as she went

163

on she lost them. She went quickly, for she had left behind her an approaching point to which she desired to return, the point of hastening death. She went peacefully, but while, days before, it had been Stanhope's intervention that had changed her mood, now she had come, by the last submissive laughter of her telephone call, into the ways of the world he had no more than opened. She went with a double watchfulness, for herself and for that other being whom her grandmother had sent her to meet, but her watchfulness did not check her speed, nor either disturb the peace. She turned, soon enough, into the street where Lawrence Wentworth's house stood, not far from the top of the Hill in one direction, from the Manor House in another, and, beyond all buildings, from the silent crematorium in a third. The street, as she came into it, looked longer than she had remembered. It had something of the effect by which small suburban byways, far inland, seem to dip towards the sea, though here it was no sea but a mere distance of road which received it. She slackened her pace, and, flicking one hand with her gloves, walked towards the house.

She reached it at last, and paused. There was at first no sign of any living creature. She looked up at it; the shadows were thick on it, seeming to expand and contract. The small occasional wind of the night, intermittently rising, caught them and flung them against it; they were beaten and bruised, if shadows could take the bruise, against its walls; they hid windows and doors; there was only a rough shape of the house discernible below them. She thought, in a faint fancy, too indistinct to be a distress, of herself flung in that steady recurrence against a bleak wall, and somehow it seemed sad that she should not be bruised. A gratitude for material things came over her; she twisted her gloves in her fingers and even struck her knuckles gently together, that the sharp feel of them might assure her of firm flesh and plotted bone. As if that slight tap had been at a door, to announce a visitor, she saw a man standing outside the shadow, close by the house.

She could not, in the moon, see very clearly what he was. She thought, by something in his form, that she had seen him before; then, that she had not. She thought of her grandmother's errand, and that perhaps here was its end. She waited, in the road, while he came down the drive, and then she saw him clearly. He was small and rather bent; obviously a working man and at that an unsuccessful working man, for his clothes were miserably old, and his boots gaped. Yet he had presence; he advanced on her with a quiet freedom, and when he came near she saw that he was smiling. He put up his hand to his tattered cap; the motion had in it the nature of an act—it had conclusion, it began and ended. He said, almost with a conscious deference such as she could have imagined herself feeling for Stanhope had she known nothing of him but his name: "Good evening, miss. Could you tell me the way to London?"

There was the faintest sound of the city's metal in his voice: dimly she knew the screech of London gate. She said: "Why, yes, but—you don't mean to walk?"

He answered: "Yes, miss, if you'll be so kind as to tell me the right road."

"But it's thirty miles," she cried, "and . . . hadn't you better. . . ." She stopped, embarrassed by the difficulties of earth. He did not look inferior enough to be offered money; money being the one thing that could not be offered to people of one's own class, or to anybody one respected. All the things that could be bought by money, but not money. Yet unless she offered this man money he did not, from his clothes, look as if he would get to London unless he walked.

He said: "I'd as soon walk, miss. It isn't more than a step."

"It seems to be considerably more," she said, and thought of her grandmother's errand. "Must you go now or could you wait till the morning? I could offer you a bed to-night." It seemed to her that this must be the reason why she was here.

He said: "I'd as soon not, though thank you for offering. I'd rather start now, if you'll tell me the way."

She hesitated before this self-possession; the idea that he needed money still held her, and now she could not see any way to avoid offering it. She looked in his serene quiet eyes, and said, with a gesture of her hand, "If it's a question of the fare?"

He shook his head, still smiling. "It's only a matter of starting right," he answered, and Pauline felt absurdly disappointed, as if some one had refused a cup of coffee or of cold water that she had wanted to bring. She was also a little surprised to find how easy it was to offer money when you tried—or indeed to take it; celestially easy. She answered his smile: "Well, if you won't . . ." she said. "Look then, this is the best way."

They walked a few steps together, the girl and the dead man, till, at a corner a little beyond Wentworth's house, she stopped.

"Down there," she said, pointing, "is the London road, you can just see where it crosses this. Are you sure you won't stay to-night and go in the morning—fare and all?" So she might have asked any of her friends, whether it had been a fare or a book or love or something of no more and no less importance.

"Quite, miss," he said, lifting his hand to his cap again in an archangelic salute to the Mother of God. "It doesn't matter perhaps, but I think I ought to get on. They may be waiting for me."

"I see," she said, and added with a conscious laughter, "One never knows, does one?"

"O I wouldn't say *never*, miss," he answered. "Thank you again. Good night, miss."

"Good night," she said, and with a last touch of the cap he was gone down the road, walking very quickly, lightly, and steadily. He went softly; she was not sure that she could hear his tread, though she knew she had not been listening for it. She watched him for a minute; then she turned her head and looked up the cross-road on the other side of the street. That way ran up towards the Manor House; she thought of her telephone call and wondered if Stanhope were asleep or awake. She looked back at the departing figure, and said after it aloud, in an act of remembered goodwill: "Go in peace!"

The words were hardly formed when it seemed to her that he stopped. The figure surely stood still; it was swaying; it was coming back—not coming back, only standing still, gesticulating. Its arms went up toward heaven in entreaty; then they fell and it bent and clutched its head with its hands. An agony had fallen on it. She saw and began to run. As she did so, she thought that her ears caught for an instant a faint sound from behind her, as of a trumpet, the echo of the trumpet of that day's rehearsal done or of the next day's performance not yet begun, or of a siren that called for the raising or lowering of a bridge.

So faintly shrill was the sound, coming to her between the cliffs of a pass from a camp on the other side the height, that her senses answered as sharply. The sound was transmitted into her and transmuted into sight or the fear of sight. "The Magus . . . my dead child . . . his own image." She was running fast; the stranger had gone an infinite distance in that time; she was running as she had run from her own room, and now she knew she had been right when she stopped, and it was a trap. Everything—she was running, for she could not stop—had been a part of the trap; even the shelter she had sometimes found had been meant only to catch her more surely in the end. Ah, the Magus Zoroaster had set it for her, all that time since, and her grandmother was part of its infinitely complicated steel mechanism, which now shut her in, and was going off—had gone off and was still going off, for ever and ever going off, in the faint shrill sound that came from behind her where Stanhope sat working it, for Zoroaster or Shelley were busy in front, and in front was the spring of the death and the delirium, and she had been tricked to run in that ingenious plot of their invention, and now she could no more stop than she could cease to hear the shrill whirr of the wheel that would start the spring, and when it cracked at last there would be her twin shape in the road. It was for this that the inhuman torturer who was Stanhope had pretended to save her, and the old creature who was her grandmother and talked of God had driven her out into the wild night, and the man who would not take her offer had fetched her to the point and the instant. Earth and sky were the climax of her damnation; their rods pressed her in. She ran; the trumpet sounded; the shape before her lifted his head again and dropped his hands and stood still.

She was coming near to him, and the only fact of peace to which her outraged mind could cling was that so far it was still he and not the other. Every second that he so remained was a relief. His back might open any moment and her own form leap hastily down from its ambush now among his veins and canals or from his interior back-throbbing heart. It did not; it became more definitely a man's back, as she neared it, but she saw it shaking and jerking. It was a great back, clothed in some kind of cloth doublet, with breeches below, and a heavy head of thick hair above; and the arms suddenly went up again, and a voice sounded. It said, in a shout of torment: "Lord God! Lord God!"

She stopped running a dozen yards off and stood still. It was not her decision; she was brought to a stand. The cry freed her from fear and delirium, as if it took over its own from her. She stood still, suddenly alert. The trap, if there had been a trap, had opened, and she had come out beyond it. But there was another trap, and this man was in it. He cried again: "Lord God!"

The trumpet had ceased blowing. She said in a voice breathless only from haste: "Can I help you?"

# The Tryst of the Worlds

The man in front became rigid: he said: "Lord God, I cannot bear the fear of the fire."

She said: "What fire?" and still with his back to her he answered: "The fire they will burn me in to-day unless I say what they choose. Lord God, take away the fear if it be thy will. Lord God, be merciful to a sinner. Lord God, make me believe."

She was here. She had been taught what to do. She had her offer to make now and it would not be refused. She herself was offered, in a most certain fact, through four centuries, her place at the table of exchange. The moment of goodwill in which she had directed to the City the man who had but lately died had opened to her the City itself, the place of the present and all the past. He was afraid, this martyr of her house, and she knew what to do. There was no doubt about it at all. She knew that the horror of the fire had overcome him. He was in the trap in which she had been but now; the universe had caught him. His teacher, his texts, his gospel had been its bars, and his judges and executioners were springing it; and the Lord God himself was, in that desperate hour, nothing but the spring that would press him into the torment. Once the Lord had been something else; perhaps still. . . . He was praying passionately: "Make me believe; make me believe." The choice was first in her; Omnipotence waited her decision.

She knew what she must do. But she felt, as she stood, that she could no more do it than he. She could never bear that fear. The knowledge of being burnt alive, of the flames, of the faces, of the prolongation of pain. She knew what she must do. She opened her mouth and could not speak. In front of her, alone in his foul Marian prison, unaware of the secret means the Lord he worshipped was working swiftly for his peace, believing and unbelieving, her ancestor stood centuries off in his spiritual desolation and preluding agony of sweat. He could not see beyond the years the child of his house who strove with herself behind and before him. The morning was

169

coming; his heart was drained. Another spasm shook him; even now he might recant. Pauline could not see the prison, but she saw him. She tried to choose and to speak.

Behind her, her own voice said: "Give it to me, John Struther." He heard it, in his cell and chains, as the first dawn of the day of his martyrdom broke beyond the prison. It spoke and sprang in his drained heart; and drove the riotous blood again through his veins: "Give it to me, give it to me, John Struther." He stretched out his arms again: he called: "Lord, Lord!" It was a devotion and an adoration; it accepted and thanked. Pauline heard it, trembling, for she knew what stood behind her and spoke. It said again: "Give". He fell on his knees, and in a great roar of triumph he called out: "I have seen the salvation of my God."

Pauline sighed deeply with her joy. This then, after so long, was their meeting and their reconciliation: their perfect reconciliation, for this other had done what she had desired, and yet not the other, but she, for it was she who had all her life carried a fear which was not her fear but another's, until in the end it had become for her in turn not hers but another's. Her heart was warm, as if the very fire her ancestor had feared was a comfort to her now. The voice behind her sang, repeating the voice in front, "I have seen the salvation of my God."

Pauline turned. She thought afterwards that she had had no choice then, but it was not so. It was a movement as swift, as instinctive, as that with which one hand flies to balance the other, but it was deliberate. She whirled on the thing she had so long avoided, and the glorious creature looked past her at the shouting martyr beyond. She was giddy with the still violence of this last evening; she shut her eyes and swayed, but she was sustained by the air about her and did not fall. She opened her eyes again; there—as a thousand times in her looking-glass—there! The ruffled brown hair, the long nose, the firm compressed mouth, the tall body, the long arms, her dress, her gesture. It wore no supernatural splendour of aureole, but its rich nature burned and glowed before her, bright as if mortal flesh had indeed become what all lovers know it to be. Its colour bewildered by its beauty; its voice was Pauline's, as she had wished it to be for pronouncing the imagination of the grand art. But no verse, not Stanhope's, not Shakespeare's, not Dante's, could rival the original, and this was the original, and the verse was but the best translation of a certain manner of its life. The glory of poetry could not outshine the clear glory of the certain fact, and not any poetry could hold as many meanings as the fact. One element co-ordinated original and translation; that element was joy. Joy had filled her that afternoon, and it was in the power of such joy that she had been brought to this closest propinquity to herself. It had been her incapacity for joy, nothing else, that had till now turned the vision of herself aside; her incapacity for joy had admitted fear, and fear had imposed separation. She knew now that all acts of love are the measure of capacity for joy; its measure and its preparation, whether the joy comes or delays.

Her manifested joy whirled on her with her own habitual movement. She sprang back from that immortality; no fear but a moment's truce of wonder and bodily tremor. She looked in her own eyes and laboured to speak; a shout was in her. She wished to assent to the choice her beatitude had made. The shout sank within her and rose without; she had assented, then or that afternoon or before this life began. She had offered her joy to her betrayed ancestor; she heard now, though she saw nothing but those brilliant and lucid eyes, the noise of his victorious going. The unseen crowd poured and roared past her. Her debt was paid, and now only she might know why and when she had incurred it. The sacrifice had been accepted. His voice was shouting in her ears, as Foxe said he had shouted, *To him that hath shall be given.* He had had; she had been given to him. She had lived without joy that he might die in joy, but when she lived she had not known and when she offered she had not guessed that the sacrificial victim had died before the sacrificial act was accomplished; that now the act was for resurrection in death. Receding voices called still; they poured onwards to the martyrdom. The confusion that was round him was her own confusion of hostile horror at the fact of glory: her world's order contending with distraction—what distraction!

One called: *What of him that hath not?* but who could be that had not? so universal, in itself and through its means, was the sublime honour of substituted love; what wretch so poor that all time and place would not yield a vicar for his distress, beyond time and place the pure vicariate of salvation? She heard the question, in that union of the centuries, with her mortal ears, as she heard excited voices round her, and the noise of feet, and the rattle at a distance of chains. She saw nothing, except the streets of the Hill and herself standing on the Hill. She felt no grief or fear; that was still to come or else it had been, according to choice of chronology. Her other self, or the image in which she saw both those choices in one vision, still stood opposite her, nor was its glory dimmed though and as her own intensity absorbed it.

After the shouted question she did not hear a reply, other sounds covered it. The scuffling, the rattling, the harsh alien voices went on; then the voice she had heard calling on the Lord cried: *The ends of the earth be upon me.* The roads had been doubled and twisted so that she could meet him there; as wherever exchange was needed. She knew it now from the abundant grace of the Hill or the hour: but exchange might be made between many mortal hearts and none know what work was done in the moment's divine kingdom. There was a pause, ominous down all the years; a suspense of silence. Then suddenly she smelt burning wood; the fire was lit, he in it. She heard the voice once more: *I have seen the salvation of my God.*

# The Tryst of the Worlds

He stood in the fire; he saw around him the uniforms—O uniforms of the Grand Duke's Guard—the mounted gentle-men, the couple of friars, the executioners—O the woodcutter's son singing in the grand art!—the crowd, men and women of his village. The heat scorched and blinded and choked him. He looked up through the smoke and flame that closed upon him, and saw, after his manner, as she after hers, what might be monstrous shapes of cherubim and seraphim exchanging powers, and among them the face of his daughter's æviternity. She only among all his children and descendants had run by a sacrifice of heart to ease and carry his agony. He blessed her, thinking her some angel, and in his blessing her æviternity was released to her, and down his blessing beatitude ran to greet her, a terrible good. The ends of the world were on them. He dead and she living were made one with peace. Her way was haunted no more.

She heard the cry, and the sky over her was red with the glow of fire, its smell in her nostrils. It did not last. Her beatitude leant forward to her, as if to embrace. The rich presence enveloped her; out of a broken and contrite heart she sighed with joy. On the inhaled breath her splendour glowed again; on the exhaled it passed. She stood alone, at peace. Dawn was in the air; *ecce omnia nova facio.*

Soon after, as she came back to the house, she saw Stanhope approaching. She waited, outside her gate. He came up, saying with a smile: "Awake, lute and harp"—he made a gesture of apology—"I myself will awake right early." She put out her hand.

"I owe you this," she said. "I owe you this for ever."

He looked at her. "It's done then?" he asked, and she: "It's done. I can't tell you now, but it's done."

He was silent, studying her, then he answered slowly: "Arise, shine; your light is come; the glory of the Lord is risen upon you." His voice quickened: "And you'll do it well, taking prettily and giving prettily, but the Lord's glory,

173

Periel, will manage to keep up with you, and I shall try."

"Oh, you!" she said, pressing and releasing his hand: "but you've got such a start!"

He shook his head. "No," he said, "our handicaps are all different, and the race is equal. The Pharisees can even catch up the woman with the mites. Those who do not insist on Gomorrah." She said: "Gomorrah?" and the chill of the word struck even through her contemplation. She remembered the unanswered question of her vision: *What of them that have not ?* As if the answer had been reserved for these lower circles, he gave it. He said: "The Lord's glory fell on the cities of the plain, of Sodom and another. We know all about Sodom nowadays, but perhaps we know the other even better. Men can be in love with men, and women with women, and still be in love and make sounds and speeches, but don't you know how quiet the streets of Gomorrah are? haven't you seen the pools that everlastingly reflect the faces of those who walk with their own phantasms, but the phantasms aren't reflected, and can't be. The lovers of Gomorrah are quite contented, Periel; they don't have to put up with our difficulties. They aren't bothered by alteration, at least till the rain of the fire of the Glory at the end, for they lose the capacity for change, except for the fear of hell. They're monogamous enough! and they've no children—no cherubim breaking into being or babies as tiresome as ours; there's no birth there, and only the second death. There's no distinction between lover and beloved; they beget themselves on their adoration of themselves, and they live and feed and starve on themselves, and by themselves too, for creation, as my predecessor said, is the mercy of God, and they won't have the facts of creation. No, we don't talk much of Gomorrah, and perhaps it's as well and perhaps not."

"But where?" she cried.

"Where but here? When all's said and done there's only

174

Zion or Gomorrah," he answered. "But don't think of that now; go and sleep if you can, or you'll be nervous this afternoon."

"Never," she said. "Not *nervous*."

"Well, that's as it may be," he said. "Still, sleep. The Sabbath and all that, even for the cattle. Be a lamb, and sleep."

She nodded, went obediently through the gate, and paused, saying: "I shall see you presently?"

"Making my concluding appearance," he said. "Unless the Lord decides to take his own call. The author has seemed to be out of the house rather often, but he may have been brought in at last. Till when, Periel, and with God."

## Chapter Ten

# THE SOUND OF THE TRUMPET

Mrs. Parry, rising that morning to control the grand occasion, and excluding from her mind as often as possible the image of a photograph in the papers of herself and Peter Stanhope side by side, "author and producer", found a note from Lawrence Wentworth waiting on her breakfast table. It was short and frigid. It said only that he had caught a feverish chill and would not be at the performance. Even so, it had given him some trouble to write, for it had demanded contact, and only a desire that he should not be, by some maddening necessary inquiry, disturbed in his solitude, had compelled him to write it. He had sent it round very early, and then had returned to sit in his study, with curtains drawn, to help him in his sickness.

"Very odd weather to catch a feverish chill," Mrs. Parry thought, looking through her window at the dancing sunlight. "And he might have returned his ticket, and he might have sent good wishes." Good wishes were precisely what Wentworth was incapable of sending anywhere, but Mrs. Parry could not know that. It was difficult to imagine what either Zion or Gomorrah would make of Mrs. Parry, but of the two it was certainly Zion which would have to deal with her, since mere efficiency, like mere being, is in itself admirable, and must be coloured with definite evil before it can be lost. She made a note to tell the Seating Committee there was a seat to spare. If there were no other absentee, if none of the cast were knocked down by a car, blown up by a geyser, or otherwise incapacitated, she would think herself fortunate. She had had a private word with Pauline the day before, after the rehearsal. Rumours of Mrs. Anstruther's condition had reached her, and she wanted, in effect, to know what Periel was going to do about it. She had always been a little worried about it, but one couldn't refuse parts to suitable people because of elderly grandmothers. Periel, however, had been entirely sensible; with the full consent, almost (Mrs. Parry understood) under the direction of the grandmother. She would, under God, be there. Mrs. Parry had not too much belief in God's punctuality, but she was more or less satisfied, and left it at that. If misadventure must come, the person best spared to it would be Peter Stanhope himself. Mrs. Parry would willingly have immolated him on any altar, had she had one, to ensure the presence of the rest, and the success of the afternoon; it was why he admired her. She desired a public success, but more ardently she desired success—the achievement. She would have preferred to give a perfect performance to empty seats rather than, to full, it should fail from perfection.

She was given her desire. Even the picture was supplied. Stanhope, approached by photographers, saw to that. He caused her to be collected from her affairs at a distance; he posed by her side; he directed a light conversation at her; and there they both were: "Mr. Stanhope chatting with the producer (Mrs. Catherine Parry)." She took advantage of the moment to remind him that he had promised to say something at the end of the play, "an informal epilogue". He assured her that he was ready—"quite informal. The formal, perhaps, would need another speaker. An archangel, or something."

"It's angelic of *you*, Mr. Stanhope," she said, touched to a new courtesy by his, but he only smiled and shook his head.

The photographs—of them, of the chief personages, of the Chorus—had been taken in a secluded part of the grounds before the performance. Stanhope lingered, watching, until they were done; then he joined Pauline.

"How good Mrs. Parry is!" he said sincerely. "Look how quiet and well-arranged we all are! a first performance is apt to be much more distracted, but it's as much as our lives are worth to be upset now."

She said thoughtfully: "She is good, but I don't think it's altogether her: it's the stillness. Don't you feel it, Peter?"

"It doesn't weigh on us," he answered, smiling, "but—yes."

She said: "I wondered. My grandmother died this morning —five minutes after I got back. I wondered if I was—imagining —the stillness from that."

"No," he said thoughtfully, "but that may be in it. It's as if there were silence in heaven—a fortunate silence. I almost wish it were the *Tempest* and not me. What a hope!

> *I'll deliver all;*
> *And promise you calm seas, auspicious gales,*
> *And sail so expeditious, that shall catch*
> *Your royal fleet far off."*

His voice became incantation; his hand stretched upward in the air, as if he invoked the motion of the influences, and the hand was magical to her sight. The words sprang over her; auspicious gales, sail so expeditious, and she away to the royal fleet far off, delivered, all delivered, all on its way. She answered: "No; I'm glad it's you. You can have your *Tempest*, but I'd rather this."

He said, with a mild protest: "Yet he wrote your part for you too; can you guess where?"

"I've been educated," she answered, brilliant in her pause before they parted. "Twice educated, Peter. Shall I try?

> *Merrily, merrily, shall I live now*
> *Under the blossom that hangs on the bough.*

Bless me to it."

"Under the Mercy," he said, and watched her out of sight before he went to find a way to his own seat.

## The Sound of the Trumpet

The theatre was almost full; late-comers were hurrying in. The gate was on the point of being closed—two minutes, as the notices had stated, before the beginning of the play—when the last came. It was Mrs. Sammile. She hurried through, and as she came she saw Stanhope. As he bowed, she said breathlessly: "So nice, isn't it? Have you got everything you want?"

"Or that we don't——" Stanhope began, but she chattered on: "But it's a good thing not to have, isn't it? Perfection would be so dull, wouldn't it? It's better to think of it than to have it isn't it? I mean, who was it said it's better to be always walking than to get there?"

"No, thank you very much," he said, laughing outright. "I'd rather have perfection than think of it, though I don't see why we shouldn't do both. But we mustn't stop; you've only a minute and a half. Where's your ticket? This way." He took her round to her seat—at the end of a row, towards the front—and as he showed it to her he said, gravely: "You won't mind getting there for once, will you? Rather than travelling hopefully about this place the whole afternoon."

She threw a look at him, as he ran from her to his own seat, which perplexed him, it seemed so full of bitterness and despair. It was almost as if she actually didn't want to sit down. He thought, as he sank into his chair, "But if one hated to arrive? if one only lived by not arriving? if one preferred avoiding to knowing? if unheard melodies were only sweet because they weren't there at all? false, false . . ." and dismissed his thought, for the Prologue stood out before the trees, and the moment of silence before the trumpet sounded was already upon them.

It sounded, annunciatory of a new thing. It called its world together, and prepared union. It directed all attention forward, as, his blasts done, the Prologue, actors ready behind and audience expectant before, advanced slowly across the grass. But to one mind at least it did even more. At the dress

179

rehearsal it had announced speech to Pauline, as to the rest; now it proclaimed the stillness. It sprang up out of the stillness. She also was aware of a new thing—of speech in relation to the silence in which it lived.

The pause in which the Prologue silently advanced exhibited itself to her as the fundamental thing. The words she had so long admired did not lose their force or beauty, but they were the mere feel of the texture. The harmony of motion and speech, now about to begin, held and was composed by the pauses: foot to foot, line to line, here a little and there a little. She knew she had always spoken poetry against the silence of this world; now she knew it had to be spoken against —that perhaps, but also something greater, some silence of its own. She recognized the awful space of separating stillness which all mighty art creates about itself, or, uncreating, makes clear to mortal apprehension. Such art, out of "the mind's abyss", makes tolerable, at the first word or note or instructed glance, the preluding presence of the abyss. It creates in an instant its own past. Then its significance mingles with other significances; the stillness gives up kindred meanings, each in its own orb, till by the subtlest graduations they press into altogether other significances, and these again into others, and so into one contemporaneous nature, as in that gathering unity of time from which Lilith feverishly fled. But that nature is to us a darkness, a stillness, only felt by the reverberations of the single speech. About the song of the Woodcutter's Son was the stillness of the forest. That living stillness had gathered the girl into her communion with the dead; it had passed into her own spirit when the vision of herself had closed with herself; it had surrounded her when she looked on the dead face of Margaret; and now again it rose at the sound of the trumpet —that which is before the trumpet and shall be after, which is between all sentences and all words, which is between and in all speech and all breath, which is itself the essential nature of all, for all come from it and return to it.

# The Sound of the Trumpet

She moved; she issued into the measured time of the play; she came out of heaven and returned to heaven, speaking the nature of heaven. In her very duty the doctrine of exchange held true, hierarchical and republican. She owed the words to Stanhope; he owed the utterance to her and the rest. He was over her in the sacred order, and yet in the sacred equality they ran level. So salvation lay everywhere in interchange: since, by an act only possible in the whole, Stanhope had substituted himself for her, and the moan of a God had carried the moan of the dead. She acted, and her acting was reality, for the stillness had taken it over. The sun was blazing, as if it would pierce all bodies there, as if another sun radiated from another sky exploring energies of brilliance. But the air was fresh.

She was astonished in the interval to hear Myrtle Fox complaining of the heat. "It's quite intolerable," Miss Fox said, "and these *filthy* trees. Why doesn't Mr. Stanhope have them cut down? I do think one's spirit needs *air*, don't you? I should die in a jungle, and this feels like a jungle."

"I should have thought", Pauline said, but not with malice, "that you'd have found jungles cosy."

"There's such a thing as being too cosy," Adela put in. "Pauline, I want to speak to you a minute."

Pauline allowed herself to be withdrawn. Adela went on: "You're very friendly with Mr. Stanhope, aren't you?"

"Yes," Pauline said, a little to her own surprise. She had rather meant to say: "O not very" or "Aren't you?", or the longer and more idiotic "Well I don't know that you'd call it friendly". But it struck her that both they and every other living creature, from the Four-by-the-Throne to the unseen insects in the air, would call it friendly. She therefore said, "Yes", and waited.

"O!" said Adela, also a little taken aback. She recovered and went on: "I've been thinking about this play. We've done so much with it—I and Mrs. Parry and the rest. . . ." She paused.

"Myrtle", Pauline said, "remarked yesterday that she felt deeply that it was so much *ours*."

"O," said Adela again. The heat was heavy on her too and she was pinker than strictly the Princess should have been. The conversation hung as heavy as the heat. A determination that had hovered in her mind had got itself formulated when she saw the deference exhibited towards him by the outer world that afternoon, and now with a tardy selfishness she pursued it. She said: "I wonder if you'd ask him something."

"Certainly—if I can decently," Pauline answered, wondering, as she heard herself use the word, where exactly the limits of decency, if any, in the new world lay. Peter, she thought, would probably find room for several million universes within those limits.

"It's like this," Adela said. "I've always thought this a very remarkable play." Pauline's heavenly nature said to her other, without irritation but with some relevance, "The hell you have!" "And," Adela went on, "as we've all been in it here, I thought it'd be jolly if we could keep it ours—I mean, if he'd let us." She realized that she hated asking favours of Pauline, whom she had patronized; she disliked subordinating herself. The heat was prickly in her skin, but she persevered. "It's not for myself so much," she said, "as for the general principle. . . ."

"O, Adela, be quick!" Pauline broke in. "What do you *want*?"

Adela was not altogether unpractised in the gymnastics of Gomorrah. Her spirit had come near to the suburbs, and a time might follow when the full freedom of the further City of the Plain would be silently presented to her by the Prince of the City and Lilith his daughter and wife. She believed— with an effort, but she believed—she was speaking the truth when she said: "I don't want anything, but I think it would be only right of Mr. Stanhope to let us have a hand in his London production."

"Us?" Pauline asked.

## The Sound of the Trumpet

"Me then," Adela answered. "He owes us something, doesn't he? and", she hurried on, "if I could get hold of a theatre—a little one—O, I think I could raise the money . . ."

"I should think you could", Pauline said, "for a play by Mr. Stanhope."

"Anyhow, I thought you might sound him—or at least back me up," Adela went on. "You do see there's nothing personal about it?" She stopped, and Pauline allowed the living stillness to rise again.

Nothing personal in this desire to clothe immortality with a career? Nothing unnatural perhaps; nothing improper perhaps; but nothing personal? Nothing less general than the dark pause and the trees and the measured movements of verse? nothing less free than interchange of love? She said: "Adela, tell me it's for yourself, only yourself, and I'll do it if I can."

Adela, extremely offended, and losing her balance said: "It isn't. We shall be as good for him as he will be for us."

"A kind of mutual-profit system?" Pauline suggested. "You'd better get back; they'll be ready. I'll do whatever you want—to-morrow."

"But——" Adela began; however, Pauline had gone; where Adela did not quite see. It was the heat of the afternoon that so disjoined movement, she thought. She could not quite follow the passage of people now—at least, off the stage. They appeared and disappeared by her, as if the air opened, and someone were seen in the midst of it, and then the air closed up, and opened again, and there was someone else. She was getting fanciful. Fortunately there was only one more act, and on the stage it was all right; there people were where she expected them. Or, if not, you could find fault; that refuge remained. She hurried to the place, and found herself glad to be there. Lingering near was the Grand Duke. He contemplated her as she came up.

"You look a little done," he said, gravely and affectionately.

"It's the heat," said Adela automatically.

"It's not so frightfully hot," Hugh answered. "Quite a good afternoon. A little thunder about somewhere, perhaps."

The thunder, if it was thunder, was echoing distantly in Adela's ears; she looked at Hugh's equanimity with dislike. He had something of Mrs. Parry in him, and she resented it. She said: "I wish you were more sensitive, Hugh."

"So long as I'm sensitive to *you*," Hugh said, "it ought to be enough. You're tired, darling."

"Hugh, you'd tell me I was tired on the Day of Judgment," Adela exclaimed. "I keep on saying it's the heat."

"Very well," Hugh assented; "it's the heat making you tired."

"I'm not tired at all," Adela said in a burst of exasperated rage, "I'm hot and I'm sick of this play, and I've got a headache. It's very annoying to be so continually misunderstood. After all, the play does depend upon me a good deal, and all I have to do, and when I ask for a little sympathy. . . ."

Hugh took her arm. "Shut up," he said.

She stared back. "Hugh——" she began, but he interrupted her.

"Shut up," he said again. "You're getting above yourself, my girl; you and your sympathy. I'll talk to you when this is over. You're the best actor in the place, and your figure's absolutely thrilling in that dress, and there's a lot more to tell you like that, and I'll tell you presently. But it's time to begin now, and go and do as I tell you."

Adela found herself pushed away. There had been between them an amount of half-pretended mastery and compulsion, but she was conscious of a new sound in Hugh's voice. It struck so near her that she forgot about Pauline and the heat and Stanhope, for she knew that she would have to make up her mind about it, whether to reject or allow that authoritative assumption. Serious commands were a new thing in their experience. Her immediate instinct was to evade: the phrase which sprang to her mind was: "I shall have to manage him—

I can manage him." If she were going to marry Hugh—and she supposed she was—she would either have to acquiesce or pretend to acquiesce. She saw quite clearly what she would do; she would assent, but she would see to it that chance never assented. She knew that she would not revolt; she would never admit that there was any power against which Adela Hunt could possibly be in a state of revolt. She had never admitted it of Mrs. Parry. It was always the other people who were in revolt against her. Athanasian in spirit, she knew she was right and the world wrong. Unathanasian in method, she intended to manage the world . . . Stanhope, Mrs. Parry, Hugh. She would neither revolt nor obey nor compromise; she would deceive. Her admission to the citizenship of Gomorrah depended on the moment at which, of those four only possible alternatives for the human soul, she refused to know which she had chosen. "Tell me it's for yourself, only yourself. . . ." No, no, it's not for myself; it's for the good of others, her good, his good, everybody's good: is it my fault if they don't see it? manage them, manage them, manage her, manage him, and them. O, the Princess managing the Woodcutter's Son, and the Chorus, the chorus of leaves, this way, that way; minds twiddling them the right way; treachery better than truth, for treachery was the only truth, there was no truth to be treacherous to—and the last act beginning, and she in it, and the heat crackling in the ground, in her head, in the air. On then, on to the stage, and Pauline was to ask Stanhope to-morrow.

Pauline watched her as she went, but she saw the Princess and not Adela. Now the process of the theatre was wholly reversed, for stillness cast up the verse and the verse flung out the actors, and though she knew sequence still, and took part in it, it was not sequence that mattered, more than as a definition of the edge of the circle, and that relation which was the exhibition of the eternal. Relation in the story, in the plot, was only an accident of need: there had been a time when it mattered, but now it mattered no longer, or for a while no longer. Presently, perhaps, it would define itself again as a need of daily life; she would be older than her master, or younger, or contemporaneous; now they were both no more than mutual perceptions in a flash of love. She had had relation with her ancestor and with that other man more lately dead and with her grandmother—all the presently disincarnate presences which lived burningly in the stillness, through which the fire burned, and the stillness was the fire. She danced out of it, a flame flung up, a leaf catching to a flame. They were rushing towards the end of the play, an end, an end rushing towards the earth and the earth rushing to meet it. The words were no longer separated from the living stillness, they were themselves the life of the stillness, and though they sounded in it they no more broke it than the infinite particles of creation break the eternal contemplation of God in God. The stillness turned upon itself; the justice of the stillness drew all the flames and leaves, the dead and living, the actors and spectators, into its power—percipient and impercipient, that was the only choice, and that was for their joy alone. She sank deeper into it. The dance of herself and all the others ceased, they drew aside, gathered up—O on how many rehearsals, and now gathered! "Behold, I come quickly! Amen, even so. . . ." They were in the groups of the last royal declamations, and swept aside, and the mighty stage was clear. Suddenly again, from somewhere in that great abyss of clarity, a trumpet sounded, and then a great uproar, and then a single voice. It was the beginning of the end; the judgment of mortality was there. She was standing aside, and she heard the voice and knew it; from the edge of eternity the poets were speaking to the world, and two modes of experience were mingled in that sole utterance. She knew the voice, and heard it; all else was still. Peter Stanhope, as he had promised, was saying a few words at the close of the play.

There was but one small contretemps. As, after moving on to the stage and turning to face the audience, Stanhope began to speak, Mrs. Sammile slid down in, and finally completely off, her chair, and lay in a heap. She had been very bright all the afternoon; in fact, she had been something of a nuisance to her immediate neighbours by the whispered comments of admiration she had offered upon the display of sound and colour before her. As the crash of applause broke out she had been observed to make an effort to join in it. But her hands had seemed to tremble and fail. Stanhope was to speak before the last calls, and the applause crashed louder when he appeared. It was in the midst of that enthusiasm that Mrs. Sammile fainted.

## Chapter Eleven

# THE OPENING OF GRAVES

Whatever mystery had, to Pauline's exalted senses, taken its place in the world on that afternoon, it seemed to make no difference to the world. Things proceeded. Her uncle had arrived from London during the performance, and had had to have his niece's absence explained to him, first by the maid and later by the niece. After the explanation Pauline remembered without surprise in her shame that she used to dislike her uncle.

Margaret Anstruther was buried on the next day but one, to the sound of that apostolic trumpet which calls on all its hearers to rise from the dead, and proclaims the creation on earth of celestial bodies, "sown in corruption, raised in incorruption; sown in dishonour, raised in glory; sown in weakness, raised in power". "Be steadfast, unmovable . . . your labour is not in vain in the Lord." Pauline heard with a new attention; these were no longer promises, but facts. She dared not use the awful phrases for herself; only, shyly, she hoped that perhaps, used by some other heavenly knowledge, they might not be altogether inapplicable to herself. The epigram of experience which is in all dogma hinted itself within her. But more than these passages another stranger imagination struck her heart: "Why are they then baptized for the dead?" There, rooted in the heart of the Church at its freshest, was the same strong thrust of interchange. Bear for others; be baptized for others; and, rising as her new vision of the world had done once and again, an even more fiery mystery of exchange rolled through her horizons, turning and glancing on her like the eyed and winged wheels of the prophet.

# The Opening of Graves

The central mystery of Christendom, the terrible fundamental substitution on which so much learning had been spent and about which so much blood had been shed, showed not as a miraculous exception, but as the root of a universal rule . . . "behold, I shew you a mystery", as supernatural as that Sacrifice, as natural as carrying a bag. She flexed her fingers by her side as if she thought of picking one up.

The funeral over, her uncle hastened action. The moment for which they had all been waiting had arrived; his mother was dead. So now they could clear things up. The house could be sold, and most of the furniture. Pauline could have a room in a London hostel, which he would find her, and a job in a London office, which he had already found her. They discussed her capacities; he hinted that it was a pity she hadn't made more of the last few years. She might have learned German while sitting with Margaret, and Spanish instead of taking part in plays. She would have to be brisker and livelier. Pauline, suppressing a tendency to point out that for years he had wished her to be not brisk or lively, but obedient and loving, said she would remember. She added that she would have a little money, enough to buy her bread. Her uncle said that a woman couldn't live on bread, and anyhow a job was a good thing; he didn't wish his niece to waste her time and energy. Pauline, thinking that Stanhope had said the same thing differently, agreed. Her uncle, having put everything he could into somebody's hands, left her to live for a few days in the house with the maid, and rushed back to London with his wife, whose conversation had been confined to assuring Pauline that she would get over it presently.

Pauline might have believed this if she had been clear what it was that she was expected to get over. Of one thing it was true; she no longer expected to see the haunting figure of her childhood's acquaintance and youthful fear. She remembered it now as one remembers a dream, a vivid dream of separation and search. She had been, it seemed, looking for a long while for someone, or perhaps some place, that was necessary to her. She had been looking for someone who was astray, and at the same time she had been sought. In the dream she had played hide-and-seek with herself in a maze made up of the roads of Battle Hill, and the roads were filled with many figures who hated—neither her nor any other definite person, but hated. They could not find anything they could spend their hate on, for they slipped and slithered and slid from and through each other, since it was their hate which separated them. It was no half-self-mocking hate, nor even an immoral but half-justified hate, certainly not the terrible, enjoyable, and angry hate of ordinary men and women. It was the hate of those men and women who had lost humanity in their extreme love of themselves amongst humanity. They had been found in their streets by the icy air of those mountain peaks of which she had once heard her grandmother speak, and their spirits had frozen in them. Among them she also had gone about, and the only thing that had distinguished her from them was her fear lest they should notice her. And while she hurried she had changed, in her bygone dream, and she was searching for some poor shadow of herself that fled into the houses to escape her. The dream had been long, for the houses had opened up, as that shadow entered, into long corridors and high empty rooms, and there was one dreadful room which was all mirrors, or what was worse than mirrors, for the reflections in those mirrors were living, though they hid for a while and had no being till the shadow at last came speeding into the room, but then they were seen, and came floating out of their flickering cells, and danced the shadow into some unintelligible dissolution among them. It was from that end that she sought to save the miserable fugitive. When in her memory she reached that point, when the shadow was fleeing deeper into Gomorrah, and she fled after it on feet that were so much swifter than its own and yet in those infinite halls and corridors could never overtake it while it fled—when the moment of approach down the last long corridor to the last utter manifestation of allusion drew near, she heard far off a trumpet, and she could remember nothing more but that she woke. She remembered that she woke swiftly, as if a voice called her, but however hard she tried she could not well recollect whose voice it was; perhaps that also was part of the dream, or perhaps it was the nurse's voice that had called her on the morning her grandmother had died. Perhaps; perhaps not. Under all the ceremonies of the days, under the companionship of her people, under her solitude, under her gradual preparations for departure and her practice of studies which were to make her more efficient in whatever job her uncle and the operation of the Immortals should find her, under sun and moon alike, she waited. She waited, and remembered only as a dream the division between herself and the glorious image by which the other was to be utterly ensouled.

It was observable, however, on the Hill, how many of the inhabitants were unwell. Mrs. Sammile had fainted, and had not been seen about since. Someone had offered to take her home in a car, but she had declined, declaring that she was all right, and had disappeared. Myrtle Fox, though she had got through the performance, had gone home crying, and had been in bed ever since. She could not sleep; a doctor had been called in, but he did not help her. She took this and that, and nothing did good. She would doze a little, and wake crying and sobbing. "It's all this excitement," her mother said severely, and opinion began to blame the play for Myrtle's illness. Lawrence Wentworth remained shut in his house; even his servants hardly saw him, and the curtains of his study were generally drawn. "It isn't human," his parlour-maid said to next door's parlour-maid. Some of the actors and some of the audience were also affected by what was generally called the local influenza epidemic. The excitement of the play or the brightness of the summer or the cold winds that even under such a sun swept the Hill, or some infection more subtle than these, struck the inhabitants down.

Neither Adela nor Hugh were among them. Hugh, like Mrs. Parry, went on efficiently dealing with the moment. Adela suffered, from the heat, from the thunder, from suppressed anxiety, but she did not go to bed. Pauline, even had she been free from her family, could not have carried out her promise, for immediately after the performance Stanhope disappeared for a few days; it was understood he had gone away for a change. Pauline could do no more than assure Adela that, as soon as he returned, she would look for an opportunity. "But I can't," she said, "do more than that. I can't butt in on him with a club, Adela. If it's for all of us, why not do it yourself? If it was for you personally, of course you might feel awkward, but as it isn't. . . ." Adela said it certainly wasn't, and went off peevishly.

As a result the management of Hugh had to be postponed. He had not, in fact, made that formal proposal which was necessary if Adela was to feel, as she wished, that she had a right and a duty to manage him. In order not to thwart him, Adela controlled herself more than was her habit when they were together. Obedience and revolt being both out of the question, she compromised temporarily that she might manage permanently. It was in such a compromise that they had been walking one evening on the Hill two or three days after Margaret Anstruther's burial. By accident, on their return, they took a road which led past the gates of the cemetery, and as they came by Hugh said idly: "I suppose Pauline'll be going now her grandmother's dead."

Adela had not thought of this. She said immediately: "O, I shouldn't wonder if she stopped—moved to a smaller house or something. She *can't* go yet."

Hugh said: "You didn't go to the funeral, darling?"

"Of course not," Adela answered. "I hate being morbid." As if to prove it she lingered to look through the gates. "There are so *many* of them," she added.

"Yes," Hugh said, with what faintly struck Adela as unnecessary obtuseness, "you can't get round death with any kind of adjective, can you?"

"I don't want to get round anything with adjectives," Adela almost snarled. "Thank God we've got away from any pretence. It's so unimportant when one doesn't pretend. When one's dead, one's dead, and that's all there is to it."

Hugh said, "Yes, but what's all there is to it? I'm that old-fashioned thing, an agnostic; I don't know. I like to be clear on what I know and what I don't know, and I don't like daydreams, either nice or nasty, or neither."

"O, nor do I," said Adela. "But you must sometimes think how nice it would be if something particular happened. I call that common sense."

"Within limits," Hugh said, putting his arm over her shoulders. "I sometimes let myself think, for a certain time, or a definite distance—say, from here to your house—how pleasant something would be—having fifty thousand pounds a year, say. But when I come to your house, or wherever it is, I stop."

"Do you?" said Adela, more impressed than she admitted to herself.

"Always," said Hugh. "And then—O, concentrate on making another fifty. Day-dreaming without limits is silly."

Adela shook her head. "I suppose I imagine rather intensely," she said. "I seem to see things *obliquely*, if you know what I mean. They're alongside the actual thing, a sort of tangent. I think really that's what all art is—tangential."

The word had hardly left her lips when a voice, tangential to her ear, said: "Do let me persuade you, Miss Hunt."

Adela, with a jump, looked round, and saw Lily Sammile. There was, at that part of the cemetery wall, a lean-to erection of boards, a kind of narrow shelter, almost a man's height, and having a rough swinging door at the nearer end. It had been there before anyone could remember, and it stayed there because no one could remember to have it taken away. It was very old and very weather-stained. It was almost a tool-shed, but then the necessary tools were, more conveniently, kept elsewhere. Everyone supposed that someone else used it. At the door of this shed, close to the cemetery railing, stood the woman who had spoken. She was leaning forward, towards Adela, and holding on to a bar of the gate. Now she put a hand on Adela's bare arm. It was gritty to the skin, which felt as if a handful of rough dust was pressed down, and pricked and rubbed it. The voice was rough too; it mumbled through a mouthful of dust. Adela pulled her arm away; she could not answer; she thrust closer to Hugh.

The woman said, after a pause during which they stared at her, and saw her dishevelled, hatless, hair of grey ashes, and cheeks almost as grey: "Come and get away. Dust—that's what you want; dust."

Hugh said easily: "Not a bit, Mrs. Sammile. We both want a great deal more."

The woman answered: "You may, but she doesn't. She's a——"

They could not catch the word, her voice so muffled it. Adela took two steps back, and said in a little squeak: "Hugh!"

Hugh slipped his arm round her. He said firmly, though less easily than before: "Well, we must be getting on. Come along, darling."

Lily Sammile began to cry. The tears ran down her face and left streaks in the greyness, as if they crept through and over grime. She said miserably: "You'll wish you had; O, you'll wish you had." She was standing with her back to the gate, leaning against it, and as she ceased to speak she became rigid suddenly, as if she listened. Her eyes widened; her nose came out over an indrawn lip; her cheeks hollowed in her effort. There was no need for the effort. They could hear the sound that held her; a faint rustle, a dry patter. It came from beyond her, and she twisted her head round—only her head— and looked. So, distracted by the movement, did the other two. They saw movement in the graves.

Most were quiet enough; their inhabitants had passed beyond any recall or return, and what influence they had on the Hill was by infection rather than by motion. But the estate was still new, and the neat ranks of sepulchres did not reach far into the enclosure. They lay along the middle path mostly; the farthest away was the mound that covered Margaret Anstruther. That too was quiet: its spirit could not conceive return. It was between the earlier graves and hers that the disclosure began, as if the enclosed space was turning itself over. The earth heaved; they felt, where they stood, no quiver. It was local, but they saw—there, and again there— the mounds swell and sway and fall in a cascade of mould, flung over the green grass. Three or four in all, dark slits in the ground, and beyond each a wide layer of dust. It did not stop there. The earth was heaving out of the dark openings; it came in bursts and rushes—in a spasmodic momentum, soon exhausted, always renewed. It hung sometimes in the air, little clouds that threatened to fall back, and never did, for they drift:d slowly to one side, and sank again on what had earlier dropped. Gravitation was reversed; the slowness and uncertainty of the movement exposed the earth's own initiation of it. The law of material things turned; somewhere in that walled receptacle of the dead activity was twisted upon itself. The backward movement of things capable of backward movement had begun. The earth continued to rise in fountains, flung up from below; and always at their height, their little height above the ground, the tops of those fountains swayed, and hurled themselves sideways, and dropped, and the rest fell back into the hidden depth of the openings, until it flung itself up once more. The gentle low patter of rough earth on gravel paths floated over the gates to the ears of the three who were still standing there.

There was a more deathly silence without the gates than within. The old woman, with twisted head, her body almost a pattern of faintly covered bones against the iron bars, was rigid; so were Adela and Hugh. They stood staring; incredulous, they gazed at the exhibited fact. So incredible was it that they did not think of the dead; ghosts and resurrections would have been easier to their minds, if more horrible, than this obvious insanity, insanity obvious in its definite existence. They were held; then, to instinctive terror, the frantic cause presented itself. Adela screamed, and as the dead man's moan had been answered in the mountain her scream was caught and prolonged in the other woman's wailing shriek. The shriek was not human; it was the wind rushing up a great hollow funnel in a mountain, and issuing in a wild shrill yell. It tore itself out of the muffled mouth, and swept over the Hill, a rising portent of coming storm. Myrtle Fox heard it in her long night of wakefulness, and her body sickened. Pauline heard it, and felt more intensely the peace that held her. Stanhope heard it, and prayed. Before the sound had died, Lily Sammile had jerked from the gate, and thrown herself at the dark shed, and disappeared within, and the swinging door fell to behind her.

As she sprang, Adela sprang also. She screamed again and ran. She ran wildly up the road, so fast that Hugh, who followed, was outdistanced. He called after her. He shouted: "Adela, it's nothing. The earth was loose and the wind was blowing. Stop." She did not stop. He kept up the pursuit down a street or two, but his own action offended him. Much though the vision had for the moment affected him, he was, as soon as he began to move, more immediately affected and angered by his situation. There might be explanations enough of what he thought he had seen—he spared a curse for Lily Sammile—but more certain than what he thought he had seen was what he knew Adela was doing. She was, faster than he, running and screaming over Battle Hill. He was angry; suppose someone met her! He raised in his own mind no reasonable pretext for abandoning her, nor did he disguise his intention from himself, but after a corner or two he simply stopped running. "Perfectly ridiculous!" he said angrily. "The earth was loose, and the wind was blowing." He was free as Pauline herself from Lilith, but without joy. There was, between the group to which his soul belonged and hers, no difference, except only that of love and joy, things which now were never to be separated in her any more.

Adela ran. She had soon no breath for screaming. She ran. She did not know where she was going. She ran. She heard a voice calling behind her: "The earth's loose and the wind's blowing", and she ran more wildly. Her flesh felt the touch of a gritty hand; a voice kept calling after her and round her: "The earth's loose; the wind's blowing." She ran wildly and absurdly, her full mouth open, her plump arms spasmodically working, tears of terror in her eyes. She desired above all things immediate safety—in some place and with someone she knew. Hugh had disappeared. She ran over the Hill, and through a twisted blur of tears and fear recognized by a mere instinct Lawrence Wentworth's house. She rushed through the gate; here lived someone who could restore her to her own valuation of herself. Hugh's shouted orders had been based on no assent of hers to authority; however much she had played at sensual and sentimental imitations of obedience, she hated the thing itself in any and every mode. She wanted something to condone and console her fear. There was a light in the study; she made for it; reached the window, and hammered on the glass, hammered again and again, till Wentworth at last heard and reluctantly drew himself from the stupor of his preoccupation, came slowly across the room and drew back the curtain.

They confronted each other through the glass. Wentworth

took a minute or two to recognize whose was the working and mottled face that confronted him, and when he recognized it, he made a motion to pull the curtain again and to go away. But as she saw the movement she struck so violently at the glass that even in his obsession he was terrified of others hearing, and slowly and almost painfully he pushed the window up and stood staring at her. She put her hands on the sill and leant inwards.

She said: "Lawrence, Lawrence, something's about!"

He still stood there, looking at her now with a heavy distaste, but he said nothing, and when she tried to catch his hand he moved it away. She looked up at him, and a deeper fear struck at her—that here was no refuge for her. Gomorrah closed itself against her; she stood in the outer wind of the plain. It was cold and frightful; she beat, literally, on the wall. She sobbed; "Lawrence, help me."

He said: "I don't know you," and she fell back, astounded. She cried out: "Lawrence, it's me, it's me, Adela. You know *me*; of course you do. Here I am—I've come to you. There's something dreadful happening and I've come to you."

He said dully: "I don't want to know you. Go away; you're disturbing me." And he moved to shut the window down.

At this she leant right forward and stared up at his eyes, for her fear desired very strongly to find that he was only defending himself against her. But his eyes did not change; they gazed dully back, so dully and so long that she was driven to turn her own away. And as she did so, sending a wild glance around the room, so urgently had she sought to find out his real desire and so strong was his rejection of her, and so fast were all things drawing to their end, that she saw, away beyond the light of the reading-lamp, a vague figure. It was in the shadows, but, as if to meet her, it thrust its head forward, and so again fulfilled its master's wish. For to Adela there appeared, stretched forward in the light, her own face, infinitely perfected in sensual grace and infinitely emptied of all meaning, even of evil meaning. Blank and dead in a spiritual death it stared vacantly at her, but undoubtedly it was she. She stood, staring back, sick and giddy at the horror, and she heard Wentworth say: "Go away; I don't want to help you; I don't know you. Go away."

He closed the window; he began to draw the curtains; the creature disappeared from her sight. And by the wall of Gomorrah she fainted and fell.

He saw her fall, and in his bemused mind he felt her as a danger to his peace. He stood looking down at her, until, slowly turning a stiff head, he saw the reflection of his doubt in the eyes of his mistress, the gleam of anxiety which reflected his own because it was concerned with himself. Reluctantly therefore he went out and half-lifted, half-dragged the girl to the gate, and got her through it, and then got her a little way down the road, and so left her lying. He mistily wondered, with a flat realism, if she would awake while he laboured, but the stupor of her horror was too deep. She lay there prone and still, and he returned.

But, as if in that effort he had slid farther down the rope of his dream, when he returned he was changed. He sat down and his creature crept up to him and took and nuzzled his hand. As she did so he became aware for the first time that he did not altogether want her. She was not less preferable than she had been for long to the real Adela, but she was less preferable now than his unimaged dream. He wanted to want her; he did not want her to go; but he could not—not as he had done. Even she was a betrayal, she was a thing outside. It was very good, as it always was, observant of his slightest wish. It sat by him, blinking at the fire. This year, in his room curtained from the sun, it was cold; he had had a fire kept up for the last few days, in spite of his servants' astonishment. He could not, as he sat, think what he wanted, unless indeed to want her, for he feared somehow to let her go: when he did he would be at the bottom of his rope. He had been given rope enough, but there was a bottom, and a dark hole, and him in the hole. He saw this dimly and was unwilling to slide lower, yet not to slide was to stop out where other things and other images were, and he was unwilling to be there also. He looked round several times, thinking that he would see something else. He thought of a girl's body lying in the road, but he could not get off his rope for that, not even if he wished, and most certainly he did not wish. Something else: something connected with his work, with the Grand Duke's Guard. What Grand Duke? The unbegotten Adela by his side said, in a low voice which stammered now as it had not before, as if it were as much losing control as was his own mind: "W-what Grand D-Duke, darling? w-what w-work?" The Grand Duke's Guard—a white square—a printed card—yes, a notice: a meaning and a message, a meeting. He remembered now. It was the annual dinner of a small historical society to which he and a few others belonged. He remembered that he had been looking forward to it; he remembered that he would enjoy going, though he could not remember for a few minutes who else came to it. He did not trouble to say anything, however; he was too tired—some drag, some pulling and thrusting had exhausted him more than he knew; he had to roll a body in the uniform of the Grand Duke's Guard, or to protect himself from hitting against its dark mass as he swung on his rope; but that was over now, and he could forget, and presently the two of them stirred and went—mumblingly and habitually—to bed.

It could not be supposed, when Adela was found soon after by a young constable on his beat, that Mr. Wentworth had had anything to do with her. The constable found her name from letters in her handbag, and presently he and others roused her people and she was got to her own temporary place, her own room. She remained unconscious till the morning; then she woke. Her temperature and her pulse were at first normal, and at first she could not recall the night. But presently it returned to her. She felt herself running again from the opening graves to the sight of the meaningless face; Hugh was running after her. Hugh was running out of the graves and driving her on to meet the face. She too, like Myrtle Fox, screamed and vomited.

Her mother rang up Hugh. There was an acrimonious conversation. Mrs. Hunt said that she had trusted Adela to Hugh's care. Hugh said that Adela had insisted on being alone, which, considering the rate at which she had run away, he felt was approximately true. Mrs. Hunt said that Adela was actually at death's door. Hugh said she would probably be wise enough not to ring the bell. Mrs. Hunt said that she herself insisted on seeing him; Adela was in no state to see anybody. Hugh said he would give himself the pleasure of leaving some flowers sometime. He knew he was behaving brutally, and that he was in fact more angry and less detached than he made his voice sound. He had left her to run, but had presently gone round and had at last reached her home in time to observe the confusion that attended her being brought home. He would have spoken, but he hated Mrs. Hunt, and he hated scenes, especially scenes at two in the morning, when his always equable passion for Adela was at ebb. So he had gone home, and indulged irritation. Nevertheless he intended to be efficient to the situation; the flowers should be taken and Adela seen that evening. He had no intention of leaving any duty unfulfilled—any duty of exterior act. He did not quite admit that there was any other kind, except in so far as outer efficiency dictated the interior.

Pursued by Hugh in her nightmares, Adela had no sense of ease or peace in his image. She ran in that recurrent flight from him through an arch that was Wentworth towards the waiting face, and as she was carried towards it, it vanished, and she was beginning again. As she ran she repeated lines and

bits of lines of her part in the play; the part she was continually
trying and continually failing to learn, the part that repeated
to her a muddle of words about perception and love which
she could never get in the right order. Sometimes Mrs. Parry
was running beside her and sometimes Mrs. Sammile; at
least, it had Mrs. Sammile's head though the body was Peter
Stanhope's, and it said as it ran: "What you want is perception
in a flash of love; what you love is a flash in a want of perception; what you flash is the want in a love of perception;
what you want is what you want . . ." and so always. Others
of her acquaintance were sometimes about her in the dream
of chaos which had but one element of identity, and that was
the race she ran and the conditions of the race. She came again
under the arch that was Wentworth, and this time there was
a change, for she found Pauline running beside her. Pauline's
hand was in hers; she clutched it, and the speed of her running
dwindled, as if a steadiness entered it. She said in a squeak:
"Pauline!"

Pauline, leaning over the bed, and feeling her hand so
fiercely held—she had called as soon as she heard Adela was
ill—said: "Yes, my dear?"

Her voice gave its full value to the last word: it rang in the
air of the dream, a billow of comprehensible sound.

Adela stopped running. She said: "Will you help me?"

"Of course," Pauline said, thinking rather ruefully of
asking Stanhope. "What do you want me to do?"

Adela said breathlessly: "I want to stop. I want to know
my part."

"But you did know your part," Pauline answered. "You
knew it beautifully, and you did it beau . . . you did it."

Adela said: "No, no; I've got to find it, and she can give it
to me."

"She?" Pauline asked.

"Lily, she . . . Sammile, whatever she's called," Adela cried.
"In the shed by the cemetery."

# The Opening of Graves

Pauline frowned. She remembered Lily Sammile very well. She remembered her as something more than an old woman by a gate, or if, then a very old woman indeed by a very great gate, where many go in who choose themselves, the gate of Gomorrah in the Plain, illusion and the end of illusion; the opposite of holy fact, and the contradiction of sacred love. She said, very quickly: "Let me run for you, Adela; you can keep quiet. I can run faster than you," she added truthfully. "I've got longer legs. Let me run instead of you. Don't worry about Mrs. ——" she could not say the name; no name was enough for the spirit that lay in Gomorrah, in the shed by the cemetery, till the graves were opened—above or below, but opened.

Adela said: "No, no; no one can do anything. She can make my head better. She can give me something. You can't do anything; you didn't see it in the house."

Pauline said: "But let's try at least. Look, let me go and learn your part." She was not quite sure, as she said it, whether this came under the head of permissible interchanges. She had meant it but for the part in the play, but this new fashion of identities was too strong for her; the words were a definition of a substitution beyond her. Adela's past, Adela's identity, was Adela's own. A god rather than she, unless she were inhabited by a god, must carry Adela herself; the god to whom baptism for the dead was made, the lord of substitution, the origin and centre of substitution, and in the sides of the mountain of the power of substitution the hermitages of happy souls restored out of substitution. A fanfare of recovered identities surrounded her; the single trumpet shrilled into diversities of music.

Adela said: "In the shed by the cemetery. I shall know my part there. Go and ask her."

Her hand shook Pauline's in her agitation, and the movement was a repulsion. Pauline, flung off upon her errand, was by the same energy repelled from her errand. Her own body

203

shook; she was tossed away from the grand gate of Gomorrah where aged Lilith incunabulates souls. She sprang up, driven by necessity, and Adela, opening her eyes which all this while had been shut, met hers. They gazed for a moment, and then Adela screamed. "Go away," she cried; "you won't, and if you do it'll be worse. You're a devil; you want me not to know. Go away; go away."

"Adela, darling," Pauline said, oblivious of repulsion in a distressed tenderness, "it's Pauline. Don't be unhappy; I'll do all I can."

"You won't, you won't," Adela screamed. "You'll spoil everything. You're torturing me; you're tearing my bones out of me; you're scraping my bones. I hate you, I hate you; go away."

Pauline heard Mrs. Hunt running up the stairs, drawn by that shriek of denial. She exclaimed, torn herself by so much pain: "I'll go, I promise. If you want——"

"No," Adela screamed, throwing her arm over her eyes, "you'll hurt us all. You don't care about us; you don't love any of us. You'll help Hugh to shut me up in the graves with it; he's got something in his room . . . it isn't me . . . it isn't . . ."

Her mother was by her, murmuring and soothing; her single look told Pauline to go, and she went. She let herself out of the house, and walked up the street, trying to settle her mind. It ought to be possible to determine what to do. Was it good for Adela, but who was to decide what was good for Adela? She—or Adela? Or someone else? Peter? but she wouldn't ask Peter, only what would he say if she did? "The Omnipotence"? Coming on the word, she considered it, and it worked upward to her freeing. She would do what Adela wanted, for it was Adela's need, and she had no reason against; she would do it in the Omnipotence, in the wood where leaves sang. Whoever was found there was subject to it, to the law of exchanged good. The Hill rose before her in the sunshine, and on its farther side the place from which her twin, now deeply one with her, had come. The mountains of impersonality have yet their hidden sides, and she was climbing towards them, in the point which was one with the universe. She knew herself going towards a thing that must be done. The growth of earth into heaven and heaven into earth approached in time a point it had already occupied in space. She could see no one else in the streets; she went lonely, and repeated to herself as she went those lines in which Peter's style individualized felicity. Up, and still up . . . where the brigands hid in a shelter and cave of the wood, and shared but did not exchange. Oh, happy and happy to have attributions of property for convenience of grace; thrice-happy that convenience of grace could dispose of property: *tam antiqua, tam nova, vita nova, nova creatura*, a new creature, no more in any sense but new, not opposed to the old, but in union with the old; new without any trick of undermeaning, new always, and now new. Up, and up, and presently down again a little; she was looking out towards the City where she was to be. She saw, away over open ground, the smoke of a train, it was carrying to the City some of those who lived or had lived upon the Hill and were leaving it or flying from it. Was the rest of the world shaken with entranced joy? Perhaps that was not discoverable, for speech of such things came only when it was permitted, and to one the world was new and to one not, to one redeemed and to one not. Yet beyond such differences there lay some act, and this was so whether or not, known or not. Perhaps to Peter to-morrow—no, to-night, for she herself must leave the Hill to-morrow, and never before had parting held such joy. Parting was a fact; all facts are joyous; therefore parting was joyous. With that unnecessary syllogism delicately exhibiting itself as a knowledge of truth, she found herself at the shed by the hill.

There it was. She had seen it a hundred times. The rough door as usual was swung to. She looked at it. This then was where Lily Sammile lived? "I could live in a nutshell and count myself king of infinite space, were it not that I have bad dreams." Was the counting of oneself king of space when one lived in a nutshell one of the bad dreams? Unheard melodies —the rigid figures on the Grecian vase? To enjoy nutshell as nutshell, vase as vase! She rapped at the door; there came no other sound. She rapped again; as if the wood thinned before her, she heard a quick breathing from within. She did not knock again; she laid a hand on the door and gently pressed.

It swung. She peered in. It was dark inside and very long and narrow and deep. Its floor slid away, hundreds of yards downward. There was no end to that floor. A little distance within the shed the woman was sitting on the earth, where the floor began to slope. She was not alone; the occupiers of the broken-up graves were with her. They were massed, mostly, about the doorway; in the narrow space there was room for infinities. They were standing there, looking at their nurse, and they were hungry. The faces—those that were still faces —were bleak with a dreadful starvation. The hunger of years was in them, and also a bewildered surprise, as if they had not known they were starved till now. The nourishment of the food of all their lives had disappeared at once, and a great void was in their minds and a great sickness. They knew the void and the sickness. The nourishment drawn from full lives had carried Margaret Anstruther and her peers over the bare mountain, and they had passed, but when the sun of the mountain struck on the people of infinite illusion it struck on all their past lives and they lived at last in the starvation they had sought. Religion or art, civic sense or sensual desire, or whatever had drugged the spirit with its own deceit, had been drawn from them; they stared famished at the dry breasts of the ancient witch. They had been freed from the grave, and had come, in their own faint presences, back to the Hill they knew, but they could not come farther on to the Hill, in the final summer of mortality, than to this mere outbuilding. Their enchantress sat there, the last illusion still with her, the illusion of love itself; she could not believe her breasts were dry. She desired infinitely to seem to give suck; she would be kind and good, she who did not depend, on whom others had depended. They stood there, but she would not see them; she who was the wife of Adam before Eve, and for salvation from whom Eve was devised after the mist had covered the land of Eden. She would not see, and she would not go to the door because of that unacknowledged crowd, but she sat there, cut off from the earth she had in her genius so long universally inhabited, gazing, waiting, longing for some of the living to enter, to ask her for oblivion and the shapes with which she enchanted oblivion. No one came; oblivion had failed. Her dead had returned to her; her living were left without her. The door swung.

Pauline saw her sitting, an old woman crouched on the ground. As the girl gazed the old woman stirred and tried to speak; there issued from her lips a meaningless gabble, such gabble as Dante, inspired, attributes to the guardian of all the circles of hell. The angelic energy which had been united with Pauline's mortality radiated from her; nature, and more than nature, abhors a vacuum. Her mind and senses could not yet receive comprehensibly the motions of the spirit, but that adoring centre dominated her, and flashes of its great capacity passed through her, revealing, if but in flashes, the single world of existence. Otherwise, the senses of her redeemed body were hardly capable yet of fruition; they had to grow and strengthen till, in their perfection, they should give to her and the universe added delight. They now failed from their beatitude, and lived neither with intuitive angelic knowledge nor immediate angelic passage, but with the slower movement of the ancient, and now dissolving, earth.

Lilith, checked in her monotonous gabble by the radiant vision who let in the sun's new light, stared at it with old and

blinking eyes. She saw the shape of the woman; and did not
know beatitude, however young. She supposed this also to be
in need of something other than the Omnipotence. She said,
separating with difficulty words hardly distinguishable from
gabble: "I can help you."

"That's kind of you," Pauline answered, "but I haven't
come to you for myself."

"I can help anyone," the old woman said, carefully enunciating the lie.

Pauline answered again: "Adela Hunt wants you." She
could and would say no more and no less. She recommended
the words to the Omnipotence (which, she thought, it was
quite certain that Adela Hunt did want, in one or both senses
of the word).

The other said, in a little shriek of alarm, such as an old
woman pretending youth might have used for girlish fun, "I
won't go out, you know. She must come here."

"She can't do that," Pauline said, "because she's ill."

"I can cure everyone," the other answered, "anyone and
everyone. You."

"Thank you very much, but I don't want anything,"
Pauline said.

The figure on the earth said: "You must. Everyone wants
something. Tell me what you want."

Pauline answered: "But I don't. You can't think how I
don't. How could I want anything but what is?"

The other made in the gloom a motion as if to crawl forward. Illusion, more lasting than in any of her victims, was in
her. At the moment of destruction she still pressed nostrums
upon the angelic visitor who confronted her. She broke again
into gabble, in which Pauline could dimly make out promises,
of health, of money, of life, or their appearances, of good looks
and good luck, or a belief in them, of peace and content, or a
substitute for them. She could almost have desired to find it
in her to pretend to be in need, to take pity, and herself to

help the thing that offered help, to indulge by her own good-will the spiritual necromancy of Gomorrah. It was not possible. The absolute and entire sufficiency of existence rose in her. She could no more herself deny than herself abandon it. She could ask for nothing but what was—life in the instant mode of living. She said: "O don't, don't."

The woman seemed to have drawn nearer, through that wriggling upon the ground; an arm poked out, and a hand clutched, too far off to catch. A voice rose: "Anything, everything; everything, anything; anything, everything; every——"

"But I don't *want* anything," Pauline cried out; and as she heard her own vain emphasis, added with a little despairing laugh: "How can I tell you? I only want everything to be as it is—for myself, I mean."

"Change," said the shape. "I don't change."

Pauline cried out: "And if it changes, it shall change as it must, and I shall want it as it is then." She laughed again at the useless attempt to explain.

At the sound of that laugh Lilith stopped, in movement and speech, and all the creatures that stood within vision turned their heads. The sterile silence of the hidden cave exposed itself, and the single laughter of the girl ran over it, and after the laughter the silence itself awoke. As if the very air emanated power, the stillness became warm; a haze of infinite specks of gold filled the darkness, as if the laughter had for a moment made its joy, and more than its joy, visible. The sombre air of the chill city of the plain was pierced by the joy of the sons of God which exists even there. Lilith shrieked and flung up her arms; and a sudden thin wail followed the shriek, the wail of all those dead who cannot endure joy. The advent of that pure content struck at the foundations of the Hill and the wail went up from all the mortal who writhed in sickness and all the immortal who are sick for ever.

## The Opening of Graves

There was a noise of cracking and breaking wood. A cloud of dust rose. Pauline threw her head back, involuntarily shutting her eyes. The dust was in her nostrils, she sneezed. As she recovered and opened her eyes, she saw that the old shed had collapsed before her. It lay, a mass of broken and discoloured wood, upon the ground. The thrust she had given to the door had been too much for it, and it had fallen.

## Chapter Twelve

## BEYOND GOMORRAH

"Then this", Stanhope said, "is a last visit?"

"Yes," Pauline said. "I'm going up to London to-morrow morning."

"You'll like the work," Stanhope went on. "Odd—to know that when you don't know what it is. You do know that?"

"Under the Mercy," she said. "I'm to see my uncle's man to-morrow at twelve, and if he approves me I shall start work at once. So then, my uncle says, I can stay with them for a few days till I've found rooms or a room."

"You'll send me the address?" he asked.

She answered: "Of course. You'll stop here still?"

He nodded, and for the minute there was silence. Then she added: "Most people seem to be trying to move."

"Most," he said, "but some won't and some can't and some needn't. You must, of course. But I think I might as well stop. There are flowers, and fruit, and books, and if anyone wants me, conversation, and so on—till the plague stops."

She asked, looking at him: "Do you know how long it will last?"

He shrugged a little: "If it's what my grandmother would have called it," he said, "one of the vials of the Apocalypse— why, perhaps a thousand years, those of the millennium before the Judgment. On the other hand, since that kind of thousand years is asserted to be a day, perhaps till to-morrow morning. We're like the Elizabethan drama, living in at least two time schemes."

She said: "It is that?"

" 'As a thief in the night'," he answered. "Could you have
a better description? Something is stealing from us our dreams
and deceptions and everything but actuality."

"Will they die?" she asked.

"I don't think anyone will die," he said, "unless—and God
redeem us all!—into the second death. But I think the plague
will spread. The dead were very thick here; perhaps that
was why it began here."

"And Adela?" she asked, "and Myrtle?"

"Why, that is for them," he answered.

But she opened on him a smile of serenity, saying: "And
for you."

"I will talk Nature to Miss Fox," he said, "and Art to Miss
Hunt. If they wish. But I think Prescott may be better for
Miss Hunt; he's an almost brutal realist, and I shall remain
a little Augustan, even in heaven."

"And I?" she asked, "I?"

"*Incipit vita nova*," he answered. "You—by the way, what
train are you catching to-morrow? I'll come and see you off."

"Half-past ten," she said, and he nodded and went on:

"You'll find your job and do it and keep it—in the City of
our God, even in the City of the Great King, and . . . and
how do I, any more than you, know what the details of Salem
will be like?"

She stood up, luxuriously stretching. "No," she said, "perhaps not. I suppose poets are superfluous in Salem?"

"I have wondered myself," he admitted. "But you needn't
realize it so quickly. If the redeemed sing, presumably someone
must write the songs. Well—I'll see you at the station to-
morrow?"

"Yes, please," she said, as they moved to the door, and
then silently down the drive under a night blazing with stars.
At the gate she gave him her hand. "It seems so funny to be
talking about trains in the easier circles of . . ." As she hesitated
he laughed at her.

"Are you afraid to name it?" he asked, and with a blush she said hastily:

". . . heaven. O good night."

"Till to-morrow and good night," he said. "Go with God."

She took two steps, paused and looked back. "Thank you for heaven," she said. "Good night."

The next morning they were on the platform together, chatting of her prospects and capacities, when as they turned in their walk Pauline said: "Peter, look—there's Mr. Wentworth. Is he coming to London too? He looks ill, doesn't he?"

"Very ill," Stanhope said gravely. "Shall we speak?" They moved down the platform, and as Wentworth turned his head in her direction Pauline smiled and waved. He looked at her vaguely, waggled a hand, and ceased. They came to him.

"Good morning, Mr. Wentworth," Pauline said. "Are you going to London too?"

He looked away from them with an action as deliberate as if he had looked at them. He said in a low mumble: "Must excuse me . . . bad chill . . . bones feel it . . . can't remember bones . . . faces . . . bones of faces, I mean."

Stanhope said: "Wentworth! *Wentworth!* . . . stop here."

The voice seemed to penetrate Wentworth's mind. His eyes crawled back along the platform, up to Stanhope's face; there they rested on the mouth as if they could not get farther than the place of the voice, they could not connect voice and eyes. He said: "Can't stop . . . must get to . . ." There, exhausted, he stopped.

Pauline heard their train coming. She said: "May I travel with you, Mr. Wentworth?"

At that he came awake; he looked at her, and then again away. He said in a tone of alarm: "No, no. Told you Guard was right. Travelling with a lady. Good-bye, good-bye," and hastily and clumsily made off up the platform as the train drew in. He scrambled into a distant compartment. Pauline sprang into her own, and turning looked at Stanhope.

"O Peter!" she said, "what's wrong?"

He had been gazing after Wentworth; he turned back to her. "I think he has seen the Gorgon's head that was hidden from Dante in Dis," he said. "Well. . . . Pray for him, and for me, and for all. You will write?"

She stretched her hand from the window. "Will I write?" she said. "Good-bye. But, Peter, ought I to do anything?"

"You can't do anything unless he chooses," he answered. "If he doesn't choose. . . . Pray. Good-bye. Go in peace."

His eyes challenged her on the word; this time she did not pause. "Go in peace," she said, "and thank you still." The train began to move; he waved to her till she was out of sight, and then went out of the station to walk in the streets and sit by the beds of Battle Hill.

Wentworth sat in his corner. He felt he had forgotten something, and slowly and laboriously he went over in his mind all that he ought to possess. He found it difficult to remember why he had left his house at all. His servants had refused to stay; they had all gone that morning; so he had had to go. He couldn't take the trouble to get others; he hadn't enough energy. He would come to London, to an hotel; there he would be quiet, and not see any ghosts. A horrible screaming ghost had looked in through his window, a ghost that had fallen down in a fit, and he had had to go out and drag it away so that other ghosts could find it. He had been afraid of them since, and of those two just now who had made mouths at him, calling him by a strange word. He was going somewhere too. He was going to a supper. He had his evening things with him in his bag. It would be necessary to dress for the supper, the supper of scholars, of historical scholars, and he was an historical scholar. He remembered what he was, if not who he was. It was true he had said the Grand Duke's Guard was correct though it wasn't, but he was an historical scholar, and he was going to his own kind of people, to Aston Moffatt.

As the name came to him, Wentworth sat up in his corner and became almost his own man again. He hated Aston Moffatt. Hate still lived in him a little, and hate might almost have saved him, though nothing else could, had he hated with a scholar's hate. He did not; his hate and his grudge were personal and obscene. In its excitement nevertheless he remembered what he had left behind—his watch. He had over-wound it weeks ago, on some day when he had seen a bad play, and had put it by to have it mended. But it was too much trouble, and now he had left it in his drawer, and couldn't tell the time. There would be clocks in London, clocks all round him, all going very quickly, because time went very quickly. It went quickly because it was unending, and it was always trying to get to its own end. There was only one point in it with which he had any concern—the time of the last supper. It would be the last supper; he would not go and meet Aston Moffatt again. But he would go to-night because he had accepted and had his clothes, and to show he was not afraid of Moffatt. That was the only time he wanted to know, the time of his last supper. Afterwards, everything would look after itself. He slept in his corner, his last sleep.

The train stopped at Marylebone, and he woke. He muddled on, with the help of a porter, to the Railway Hotel. He had thought of that in the train; it would save bother. He usually went to some other, but he couldn't remember which. The ordinary habits of his body carried him on, and the automatic habit of his mind, including his historic automatic. History was his hobby, his habit; it had never been more. Its austerity was as far from him now as the Eucharists offered in the Church of St. Mary la Bonne, or the duties of the dead, or the ceremonies of substituted love. He automatically booked a room, ate some lunch, and then lay down. This time he did not sleep; the noise of London kept him awake; besides he was alone. The creature that had been with him so long was with him no more. It had gone upstairs with him for the last time two nights before, and had his former faculties lived he would have seen how different it was. After the passage of the dead man it had never quite regained its own illusive apparition; senility and youth had mingled in its face, and in their mingling found a third degree of corruption. At the hour of the falling in of the shed of Lilith it had thinned to a shape of twilight. Meaning and apparent power had gone out of it. It was a thing the dead man might have met under his own pallid sky, and less even than that. In the ghostly night that fell on the ruins of Gomorrah it had tottered round its father and paramour, who did not yet know through what destruction they went. His eyes were dimmed. Those who look, in Stanhope's Dantean phrase, on the head of the Gorgon in Dis, do not know, until Virgil has left them, on what they gaze. In the night she was withdrawn; the substance of illusion in her faded, and alongside his heavy sleep she changed and changed, through all degrees of imbecile decay, till at last she was quite dispelled.

He was alone. He lay awake, and waking became aware of his ancient dream. Now he was near the end of his journey. He saw below him the rope drawn nearer and nearer to the wall, if it were a wall. He looked up; above him the rope seemed to end in the moon, which shone so fully in the dark, millions of miles away. Down all those miles he had slowly climbed. It was almost over now; he was always a little lower, and when he stood up he did not lose the dream. Through his bathing and dressing and going down and finding a taxi he was still on his rope. He felt once for his watch, and remembered he had not got it, and looked up at the shining silver orb above, and found that that was his watch. It was also a great public clock at which he was staring; but he could not make it out—moon or watch or clock. The time was up there; but he could not see it. He thought: "I shall be just in time."

He was, and only just; as close to its end as to the end of the rope.

He got into his taxi. It went off along the High Street, and then was held up behind a policeman's arm. He was looking out of the window, when he thought a creaking voice said in his ear, as if a very old woman was in the seat beside him: "Madame Tussaud's." He did not look round, because no one was ever there, but he stared at the great building which seemed to glow out of the darkness of the side of the abyss, and there rose in him the figure of what it contained. He had never been there, though in a humorous moment he had once thought of taking Adela, but he knew what was in it—wax images. He saw them—exquisitely done, motionless, speechless, thoughtless; and he saw them being shifted. Hanging on his rope, he looked out through the square of light in the darkness and saw them all—Cæsar, Gustavus, Cromwell, Napoleon, Foch, and saw himself carrying them from one corner to another, and putting them down and picking them up and bringing them somewhere else and putting them down. There were diagrams, squares and rectangles, on the floor, to show where they should go; and as he ran across the hall with a heavy waxen thing on his shoulder he knew it was very important to put it down in the right diagram. So he did, but just as he went away the diagram under the figure changed and no longer fitted, and he had to go back and lift the thing up and take it off to another place where the real diagram was. This was always happening with each of them and all of them, so that six or seven or more of him had to be about, carrying the images, and hurrying past and after each other on their perpetual task. He could never get the details correct; there was always a little thing wrong, a thing as tiny as the shoulder-knots on the uniforms of the Grand Duke's Guard. Then the rope vibrated as the taxi started again, and he was caught away; the last vestige of the history of men vanished for ever.

Vibration after vibration—he was very near the bottom of his rope. He himself was moving now; he was hurrying. The darkness rushed by. He stopped. His hand, in habitual action, had gone to his pocket for silver, but his brain did not follow it. His feet stepped, in habitual action, off the rope, on to the flat ground. Before him there was a tall oblong opening in the dark, faintly lit. He had something in his hand—he turned, holding it out; there was a silver gleam as it left his hand, and he saw the whole million-mile-long rope vanishing upward and away from him with incredible rapidity towards the silver moon which ought to have been in his waistcoat pocket, because it was the watch he had overwound. Seeing that dazzling flight of the rope upwards into the very centre of the shining circle, he thought again: "I'm just in time." He was standing on the bottom of the abyss; there remained but a short distance in any method of mortal reckoning for him to take before he came to a more secret pit where there is no measurement because there is no floor. He turned towards the opening and began his last journey.

He went a little way, and came into a wider place, where presently there were hands taking off a coat he discovered himself to be wearing. He was looking at himself; for an instant he had not recognized his own face, but he did now, over a wide shining oval thing that reminded him of the moon. He was wearing the moon in front of him. But he was in black otherwise; he had put on a neat fantastic dress of darkness. The moon, the darkness, and he—only no rope, because that had gone away, and no watch, because he had done something or other to it, and it had gone away too. He tried to think what a watch was and how it told him the time. There were marks on it which meant something to do with time, but he didn't know what. Voices came to him out of the air and drove him along another corridor into another open space. And there suddenly before him was Sir Aston Moffatt.

## Beyond Gomorrah

The shock almost restored him. If he had ever hated Sir Aston because of a passion for austere truth, he might even then have laid hold on the thing that was abroad in the world and been saved. If he had been hopelessly wrong in his facts and yet believed them so, and believed they were important in themselves, he might have felt a touch of the fire in which the Marian martyr had gone to his glory, and still been saved. In the world of the suicides, physical or spiritual, he might have heard another voice than his and seen another face. He looked at Sir Aston and thought, not "He was wrong in his facts", but "I've been cheated". It was his last consecutive thought.

Sir Aston was decidedly deaf and extremely talkative, and had a sincere admiration for his rival. He came straight across to Wentworth, and began to talk. The world, which Wentworth had continuously and persistently denied in favour of himself, now poured itself over him, and as if in a deluge from heaven drove him into the depths. Very marvellous is the glorious condescension of the Omnipotence; the myth of the fire which was rained over the plain now incarnated itself in Sir Aston Moffatt. Softly and gently, perpetually and universally, the chatty sentences descended on the doomed man, each sentence a little prick of fire, because, as he stood there, he realized with a sickness at heart that a voice was talking and he did not know what it was saying. He heard two sounds continually repeated: "Went-worth, Went-worth." He knew that those two noises meant something, but he could not remember what. If all the faces that were about him would go away he might remember, but they did not go. They gathered round him, and carried him forward in the midst of them, through a doorway. As he went through it he saw in front of him tables, and with a last flash of memory knew that he had come there to eat and drink. There was his chair, at the bottom left corner, where he had always sat, his seat in the Republic. He went to it with an eager trot. It was waiting

for him as it had always waited, for ever and ever; all his life
and from the creation of the world he had sat there, he would
sit there at the end, looking towards the—he could not think
what was the right name for the tall man at the other end,
who had been talking to him just now. He looked at him and
tried to smile, but could not, for the tall man's eyes were
blank of any meaning, and gazed at him emptily. The
Republic deserted him. His smile ceased. He was at last by
his chair; he would always sit there, always, always. He sat
down.

As he did so, he knew he was lost. He could not understand
anything about him. He could just remember that there had
been one moment when a sudden bright flash had parted from
him, fleeing swiftly across the sky into its source, and he wanted
that moment back; he wanted desperately to hold on to the
rope. The rope was not there. He had believed that there
would be for him a companion at the bottom of the rope
who would satisfy him for ever, and now he was there at the
bottom, and there was nothing but noises and visions which
meant nothing. The rope was not there. There were faces,
which ceased to be faces, and became blobs of whitish red
and yellow, working and twisting in a horrible way that yet
did not surprise him, because nothing could surprise him.
They moved and leaned and bowed; and between them were
other things that were motionless now but might at any moment
begin to move and crawl. Away over them was a huge round
white blotch, with black markings on it, and two long black
lines going round and round, one very fast and one very slow.
This was time, too fast for his brain, too slow for his heart.
If he only had hold of the rope still, he could perhaps climb
out of this meaningless horror; at least, he could find some
meaning and relation in it all. He felt that the great blotch
had somehow slid up and obscured the shining silver radiance
into which a flash out of him had gone, and if he could get
the rope he could climb past, or, with great shuddering, even

through the horrible blotch, away out of this depth where anything might be anything, and was anything, for he did not know
what it was. The rope was not there.

He shrank into himself, trying to shut his eyes and lose
sight of this fearful opposite of the world he had known. Quite
easily he succeeded. But he could not close his ears, for he
did not know how to manage the more complex co-ordination
of shoulders and arms and hands. So there entered into him
still a small, steady, meaningless flow of sound, which stung
and tormented him with the same lost knowledge of meaning;
small burning flames flickered down on his soul. His eyes
opened again in mere despair. A little hopeless voice came
from his throat. He said, and rather gasped than spoke: "Ah!
ah!" Then everything at which he was looking rushed together and became a point, very far off, and he also was a
point opposite it; and both points were rushing together,
because in this place they drew towards each other from the
more awful repulsion of the void. But fast as they went they
never reached one another, for out of the point that was not
he there expanded an anarchy of unintelligible shapes and hid
it, and he knew it had gone out, expiring in the emptiness
before it reached him. The shapes turned themselves into
alternate panels of black and white. He had forgotten the
name of them, but somewhere at some time he had thought
he knew similar forms and they had had names. These had
no names, and whether they were or were not anything, and
whether that anything was desirable or hateful he did not
know. He had now no consciousness of himself as such, for the
magical mirrors of Gomorrah had been broken, and the city
itself had been blasted, and he was out beyond it in the blank-
ness of a living oblivion, tormented by oblivion. The shapes
stretched out beyond him, all half turned away, all rigid and
silent. He was sitting at the end, looking up an avenue of
nothingness, and the little flames licked his soul, but they did
not now come from without, for they were the power, and the

only power, his dead past had on him; the life, and the only life, of his soul. There was, at the end of the grand avenue, a bobbing shape of black and white that hovered there and closed it. As he saw it there came on him a suspense; he waited for something to happen. The silence lasted; nothing happened. In that pause expectancy faded. Presently then the shape went out and he was drawn, steadily, everlastingly, inward and down through the bottomless circles of the void.